HOUGHTON MIFFLIN HARCOURT

WRITE SOURCE

GREAT
SOURCE.

HOUGHTON MIFFLIN HARCOURT

A Few Words About the *Write Source SkillsBook*

Before you begin . . .

The *SkillsBook* provides you with opportunities to practice the editing and proofreading skills presented in the *Write Source* textbook. The textbook contains guidelines, examples, and models to help you complete your work in the *SkillsBook*.

Each *SkillsBook* activity includes a brief introduction to the topic and refers you to the pages in the textbook that offer additional information and examples. The "Proofreading Activities" focus on punctuation and the mechanics of writing. The "Parts of Speech Activities" highlight each of the eight parts of speech. The "Sentence Activities" provide practice in sentence combining and in correcting common sentence problems.

The Extend

Many activities include an **Extend** at the end of the exercise. Its purpose is to provide ideas for follow-up work that will help you apply what you have learned to your own writing.

Printed in the U.S.A.

ISBN-13 978-0-547-48465-5

3 4 5 6 7 8 9 10 0928 17 16 15 14 13 12

4500358513   A B C D E F G

CONTENTS
Proofreading Activities

Editing for Mechanics

Using the Right Word

Parts of Speech Activities

Nouns

Pronouns

Verbs

Adjectives & Adverbs

Prepositions, Conjunctions, & Interjections

Sentence Activities

Sentence Basics

Proofreading Activities

The activities in this section of your *SkillsBook* include sentences that need to be checked for punctuation, mechanics, or correct word choices. Most of the activities also include helpful textbook references. In addition, the **Extend** activities provide follow-up practice of certain skills.

Pretest: Punctuation

> **Add** the missing periods, question marks, exclamation points, commas, semicolons, apostrophes, and hyphens. Capitalize the first word of each sentence.

1   My grandmother was born in 1900 in a small, poor village near the

2   Italian-Swiss border. she was the first daughter to survive infancy and

3   her parents always treated her like a very special gift when she was nine

4   years old her family immigrated to the United States they hoped that the

5   golden shores of America would offer the opportunities and advantages so

6   lacking in their own country

7   during their arduous ocean voyage one of my grandmothers younger

8   brothers died of dysentery the parents were heartbroken however they

9   chose to view his death as a symbol of rebirth for the entire family the

10   ship docked at Ellis Island which lies off the shores of New York City

11   here their papers were processed and doctors examined everyone for

12   communicable diseases did they receive a clean bill of health indeed they

13   did they were allowed to depart for the mainland

14   in 1910 eight long months after leaving Europe the family finally

15   arrived in San Francisco here they set up house and began their new life

16   San Francisco was very good to them my great grandfather immediately

17   purchased 200 acres of land in the Napa Valley he planted grapes and

18   began the slow demanding process of developing a winery the entire

19   family became involved in this endeavor and within five years their efforts

20   were repaid the fertile vineyards which produced some of the finest wines

21   in northern California are still in use today

4

> **Write T** before each true statement. Write **F** if the statement is false.

_____F_____ **1.** A semicolon is the punctuation mark generally used between two independent clauses that are joined by a coordinating conjunction.

_____ **2.** A comma should separate an adverb clause or a long modifying phrase from the independent clause that follows it.

_____ **3.** A comma usually precedes the opening quotation marks in a line of dialogue, setting off the speaker's words from the rest of the sentence.

_____ **4.** A comma may be used to join independent clauses that are not connected with a coordinating conjunction.

_____ **5.** Semicolons are used to separate lists or groups of words that already contain commas.

_____ **6.** A colon may be used to introduce a list.

_____ **7.** Underlining (italics) is used to punctuate titles of songs, poems, short stories, lectures, episodes of radio or television programs, chapters of books, unpublished works, and articles found in magazines, newspapers, or encyclopedias.

_____ **8.** Periods and commas should be placed inside quotation marks.

_____ **9.** The possessive form of singular nouns is usually made by adding an apostrophe and an *s*.

_____ **10.** The hyphen is used correctly in these words: T-shirt, U-turn, x-axis.

_____ **11.** Common conjunctive adverbs include *besides, however, instead, meanwhile, then,* and *therefore.*

_____ **12.** A semicolon is used before a conjunctive adverb when the word connects two independent clauses in a compound sentence.

_____ **13.** Commas are used to enclose restrictive phrases and clauses.

_____ **14.** Commas are used correctly in this sentence: The banquet, which was held to honor her 60th birthday, was a surprise.

_____ **15.** Commas are used to separate coordinate adjectives that equally modify the same noun.

End Punctuation

Three different punctuation marks are used to end sentences: the period, the question mark, and the exclamation point. As you know, each indicates something different. Turn to 605.1, 605.4, and 606.1 in *Write Source*.

> **Add** a period, a question mark, or an exclamation point at the end of each of the following sentences. Capitalize letters as needed.

1   Have you ever asked yourself, "what is time? is time travel possible"

2   these questions have intrigued scientists and philosophers throughout the

3   ages time is still very difficult to define just check any dictionary, and

4   you'll discover that time is explained in relation to something else—an

5   event, a distance, or some other concept

6   Albert Einstein's theory of relativity ($E=mc^2$) showed that theoretically

7   time travel was possible Einstein talked about "spacetime," a four-

8   dimensional "fabric" created when time and space come together another

9   scientist has even claimed, "I can describe how to build a time machine

10   that adheres to the laws of physics" (remember, these laws tell us what is

11   possible, not what is currently practical)

12   By now, you're probably asking, "how is time travel possible" an

13   object traveling at an exceptionally high speed ages more slowly than a

14   stationary object this means that if you could travel into outer space at

15   a velocity approaching the speed of light, you would actually age more

16   slowly than people on earth could you travel into the past (think of the

17   incredible changes you could make) physicists haven't envisioned a way to

18   make this happen—not yet, anyway

Extend: Write three to five statements about something fantastic you think could happen in the future. Use each of the three end punctuation marks at least once.

Review: End Punctuation

> **Add** a period, a question mark, or an exclamation point at the end of each sentence. Capitalize letters as needed.

1 How "fast" is high-speed travel? you might say, "it depends on

2 your point of view"—and you're right for centuries, the stagecoach was

3 considered the ultimate transport at 10 mph in the mid-1800s, you could

4 zoom about on the early railroads—at 25 mph around 1915, if you owned

5 an automobile, you could zip along at 50 mph

6 The first airplanes took off in the early 1900s, flying rather shakily

7 at 30 mph in 1939, the first jet cruised the skies at 435 mph eight years

8 later, Chuck Yeager broke the sound barrier (758 mph) when his X-1 hit

9 810 mph Yeager's X-1 was a turtle compared to the *Apollo* spacecraft—

10 which ferried astronauts to the moon at 20,000 mph

11 What does the future hold new energy sources might make speedier

12 spaceships possible Dr. W. A. Shinghton says, "an antimatter fusion ship

13 might run off energy released from matter-antimatter destruction, the most

14 powerful force in the universe an engine using this kind of energy," Dr.

15 Shinghton continues, "could send a ship into space at 225,000 mph"

16 What about "warp speed" light is the fastest thing in our universe, yet

17 it takes light from the nearest star four years to reach Earth Dr. Shinghton

18 explains, "a warp drive would compress spacetime in front of a ship and

19 expand spacetime behind it, making a starship zip through the warp

20 faster than light speed" it's possible that someday we will easily explore

21 the entire universe and go where no man—or woman—has gone

22 before

Commas Between Independent

You may join two independent clauses usi_____ a coordinating conjunction (*and, but, or, nor, for, yet,* and *so*). See 608.1 and 7_____ _rce.

> **Join** each pair of sentences wit_____ a coordinating conjunction. Choose the conjunction that you think is

1. Castles offer a window_____ _l times, *and* They inspire tales of knights and valor.

2. People began building castles in the ninth century. Those early efforts bore little resemblance to King Arthur's castle in Camelot.

3. Most early castles were constructed of wood. It was not until the 1100s that builders of castles used stone.

4. Some people built castles on lakes, riverbanks, mountaintops, or steep hillsides. These settings provided natural defenses.

5. As time progressed, castles became larger. They included more advanced defensive features.

6. One example, the arrow slit, allowed an archer to shoot out of a small window. The window was so small that an attacker could not shoot in.

7. Tradespeople and peasants were not allowed to live in the nobleman's castle. They built their homes outside its walls, creating towns.

8. Some castles were almost impenetrable. A clever enemy could still find weaknesses.

9. Attackers might dig under the walls to make them collapse. They might choose a slower assault: surrounding the castle and waiting for the inhabitants to run out of food.

Extend: Turn to page 600 in *Write Source*. Read the information pertaining to an allusion. Join the two sentences in the example using a comma and an appropriate coordinating conjunction. Write three allusions of your own using commas and coordinating conjunctions.

Commas

Use commas to separate words and phrases in a series and to separate equal adjectives. Turn to 608.2 and 610.2 in *Write Source*.

> **Use** commas to separate items in a series and to separate equal adjectives as you combine each pair of sentences below.

1. One of the most fascinating rivalries in ancient Greece was between Sparta and Athens. It was also one of the oldest rivalries.

One of the oldest, most fascinating rivalries in ancient Greece was

between Sparta and Athens.

2. Sparta had strict discipline and great warriors. Sparta also had a strong ruling class.

3. Athens was known for its tremendous wealth. It was also known for its great artists and its powerful navy.

4. In 431 B.C.E., the Peloponnesian War broke out; the war involved Sparta and Athens. Their allies fought, too.

5. Ten years later, this war ended in a stalemate. This war was deadly and costly.

6. In 415 B.C.E., Athens attacked again, but Sparta's army eventually won. Sparta's army was strong and well disciplined.

Extend: Write two sentences in which you use commas to separate words in a series and commas to separate equal adjectives.

Commas After Introductory Phrases & Clauses 1

A comma is used to separate an introductory word group from the rest of the sentence. Introductory word groups are usually clauses or phrases. Turn to 610.3 and 614.1 in *Write Source*. Read the examples carefully. Often, you can sense when the introductory material ends and the main idea begins, but it also helps to be able to identify phrases and clauses. Turn to pages 742 and 744 for more information about phrases and clauses.

> **Add** commas to separate introductory information from the rest of the sentence.

1 During the Second World War, women played an active role in the

2 armed forces. After Pearl Harbor was attacked American factories more

3 than doubled their production of aircraft. As a matter of fact they cranked

4 out 48,000 planes in 1942 alone. Thousands of these planes had to be

5 flown from the factories to air bases. Because male pilots were fighting

6 abroad there was a shortage of pilots in the states.

7 More than 1,000 women volunteered to become pilots for the Women

8 Airforce Service Pilots (WASPs). They received the same instruction as

9 male pilots. During their 200 hours of flight school and 600 hours of

10 ground school they studied physics, navigation, flight theory, and Morse

11 code.

12 After they graduated WASPs went to air bases across the country.

13 By the summer of 1943 they were ferrying aircraft throughout the United

14 States. They flew seven days a week and had to be ready for anything.

15 One pilot left on a ferrying trip that was to take one day. After flying

16 17,000 miles in 30 days she returned to the base in the same clothes

17 she had on when she left. Although most missions involved flying in

18 noncombat zones 38 women pilots died in the line of duty.

Extend: Write two sentences; use an introductory phrase in one and introductory clause in the other.

Commas After Introductory Phrases & Clauses 2

Introductory phrases and clauses are usually set off from the rest of the sentence with a comma. By reading carefully, you will sense when the introductory material ends and the main sentence begins. Place a comma at that point. Turn to 610.3 in *Write Source*. Read the examples, pausing at the commas. For information about clauses and phrases, turn to pages 742 and 744.

> **Insert** commas wherever they are needed to separate introductory information from the rest of the sentence.

1   After Amelia Earhart disappeared in 1937, Jackie Cochran became one

2 of America's most famous female pilots. In just 10 years Cochran set 17

3 world records in aviation. On September 23, 1938 her silver P-35 flashed

4 across the finish line in the challenging Bendix Race. Completing the

5 2,042 miles from Los Angeles to Cleveland she became the first pilot to

6 finish the race nonstop in just over eight hours.

7   Born Bessie Mae Pittman somewhere in the South Jackie Cochran was

8 raised by a foster family. In her autobiography she remembers having no

9 shoes and wearing dresses made of flour sacks. As a teenager she learned

10 how to cut hair and then headed north. On her way to New York City

11 she picked the name Jacqueline Cochran out of a phone book and decided

12 to reinvent herself. "I might have been born in a hovel," she recalled, "but

13 I was determined to travel with the wind and the stars." At the same

14 time she worked in a New York beauty salon Jackie learned to fly. "At the

15 moment I paid for my first lesson a beauty operator ceased to exist and

16 an aviator was born."

17   Meanwhile, in nearby Boston, a young woman began a career selling

18 airplanes. From a prominent Philadelphia family the young saleswoman,

19 Nancy Harkness, married Air Corps Reserve officer Robert Love.

20   As the daughter of a wealthy physician Nancy Harkness learned to

21   fly as a teenager. Though she went to the very best schools she remained

22   restless and adventurous. While she was in college she earned extra

23   money by taking students for airplane rides. When she flew too low over

24   the campus university officials were not amused and suspended her from

25   school for two weeks.

26   After their marriage the Loves formed an aviation company. Nancy

27   flew for that company and also flew for the Bureau of Air Commerce. In

28   one of the bureau's projects she tested the three-wheeled landing gear,

29   which became standard on most planes.

30   Both Nancy Harkness Love and Jackie Cochran had the same

31   vision—to form a group of women pilots that would ferry needed military

32   aircraft to air bases. In the spring of 1942 the Women's Auxiliary

33   Ferrying Squadron (WAFS) began training under Nancy Harkness Love.

34   Shortly after that Jackie Cochran's group of flying cadets also began

35   training. Ten months later the WAFS and Cochran's trainees merged into

36   the Women Airforce Service Pilots (WASPs). During the Second World War

37   WASPs flew more than 60 million miles in every type of military plane.

Explain in your own words how you determine where you should use commas to separate introductory information from the rest of the sentence.

_____

_____

_____

_____

Review: Commas 1

Insert commas where they are needed in the sentences below. Write the rule for each comma you insert.

1. Although the brain comprises only 2 percent of a person's total body weight, it requires 20 percent of all oxygen used by the body.

   Rule: _Use a comma after an introductory clause._

2. My orthodontist will explain to my parents the cost of a retainer the need for it and the way I am to use it.

   Rule: _____

3. I have taken science courses all through high school and I expect to major in chemistry at the University of Wisconsin.

   Rule: _____

   _____

4. The tiny delicate hummingbird weighs less than a penny and it is the only bird—believe it or not—that can fly backwards.

   Rule: _____

   Rule: _____

   _____

5. The hummingbird has a body temperature of 111 degrees Fahrenheit beats its wings more than 60 times a second and builds a nest the size of a walnut.

   Rule: _____

6. Even though the hummingbird is hard to see it can often be spotted around red flowers or red feeders.

   Rule: _____

Commas to Set Off Contrasted Elements & Appositives

Contrasted elements usually begin with *not, but, but not, though,* or *unlike* and should be set off with commas. Turn to 608.3 in *Write Source*. An appositive is a word or a phrase that identifies or renames the noun or pronoun that comes before it. Turn to 610.1.

> **Add** commas where they are needed in the sentences below.

1. Sir Arthur Conan Doyle created Sherlock Holmes , one of the world's best-known detectives.

2. Dr. Watson Holmes's sidekick and friend helped solve cases.

3. Sherlock Holmes always got his man not by force but through amazing use of reason and observation.

4. In 1893, Doyle wrote a story in which Holmes the great detective was killed.

5. The outcry of millions of readers all devoted fans convinced Doyle to bring Holmes back to life in another story.

6. Sir Doyle perhaps the most highly paid short-story writer of his time came to resent Holmes's fame.

7. Doyle grew agitated because Holmes his best-known character diverted attention from what Doyle considered to be his most serious literary effort historical novels.

8. Christopher Morley an English critic said about Holmes, "Perhaps no fiction character ever created has become so charmingly real to his readers."

9. Medicine not writing was Doyle's original profession; he trained as a doctor.

Extend: Write three to five sentences about one of your favorite fictional characters. Include one appositive or contrasted element in each sentence.

Commas with Nonrestrictive Phrases & Clauses 1

A nonrestrictive phrase or clause adds information that is not necessary to the basic meaning of the sentence, so it is set off with commas. If a sentence has the same meaning with or without it, the clause or phrase is nonrestrictive. Turn to 642.2 in *Write Source*.

> **The Marshall Islands, a country in the North Pacific Ocean, consists of 29 atolls and 5 islands.** (The phrase is not necessary.)

> **The Marshall Islands consists of 29 atolls and 5 islands.**
> (The sentence has the same meaning without the nonrestrictive phrase.)

Place commas around the nonrestrictive phrases and clauses in the sentences below. Underline restrictive phrases or clauses.

1. The land area of the Marshall Islands, which covers only about 70 square miles, is scattered over 780,000 square miles.

2. The nationality that makes up most of the country's population is Micronesian.

3. About 30,000 people half of the country's population live on Majuro Atoll.

4. The rural areas where a traditional way of life is maintained are home to 30 percent of the people.

5. People who reside in the urban areas live with the modern conveniences of electricity, telephones, and television.

6. The islands which were controlled by Germany from 1886 until 1914 and by Japan until 1944 became a United States territory during World War II.

7. Bikini Atoll is famous for nuclear testing conducted by the U.S. military from 1946–1958 that resulted in the resettling of natives to other islands.

8. Ten years later, some people returned to the atoll which was declared safe from harmful radiation in 1968.

9. But 10 years after that, government officials finding unsafe radiation levels resettled the people again.

Commas with Nonrestrictive Phrases & Clauses 2

Commas are used to enclose nonrestrictive phrases and clauses. Nonrestrictive phrases and clauses are those that are not essential to the basic meaning of the sentence. Turn to 612.2 in *Write Source*.

> **Place** commas around each nonrestrictive phrase or clause in the following sentences. Underline restrictive phrases or clauses.

1. If you go to New York City, which is one of the most interesting places on earth, you should visit the New York Botanical Garden.

2. My grandmother who was recently diagnosed with diabetes must watch how much sugar she eats.

3. The neighbor who lives east of us has many bowling trophies.

4. The island of Sri Lanka formerly called Ceylon is one of the most densely populated areas on Earth.

5. The invention of the videocassette recorder which some feared would bring about the demise of movie theaters has not adversely affected box-office sales in the slightest.

6. The field mouse trying to escape a swooping hawk disappeared into a hole in the barn's siding.

7. The ancient cherry tree a cherished part of the town's history became diseased and had to be cut down.

8. The ladder that has a rung missing could be dangerous to use.

9. People who wanted to buy this year's popular toy had to get to the store before it opened and wait in line.

10. Memorial Day when the Indianapolis 500 race is held is a national day meant to remember soldiers.

Extend: Look for four examples of nonrestrictive phrases or clauses in newspapers, books, or magazines. Be prepared to share your examples with a learning partner or your class.

Other Uses of Commas 1

Use commas to set off items in a date, items in an address, dialogue, nouns of direct address, and interjections. See 614.2, 616.1, 616.2, and 616.4 in *Write Source*.

> **Add** commas where they are needed in the sentences below. Write the rule that applies in each case.

1. Drat, Bill forgot to get my English assignment from Mr. Taylor.

Rule: *Commas set off an interjection or a weak exclamation from the rest of the sentence.*

2. "I reminded you Bill to get my assignment," I spouted.

Rule: _____

_____

3. "I just forgot" Bill mumbled in apology.

Rule: _____

4. "Jeepers how could you forget something important like that?" I asked.

Rule: _____

_____

5. I told Bill that I would be visiting my grandmother beginning November 7 2011 and that he could e-mail the assignment or send it to me at 168 State Street Albany New York 12205.

Rule: _____

Rule: _____

6. "I'll do my best" Bill replied.

Rule: _____

7. I said "I will appreciate your help a lot."

Rule: _____

Extend: Write a sentence for each of the five comma uses covered in this exercise.

Other Uses of Commas 2

Use commas to set off interruptions, to separate numerals in large numbers, to enclose titles or initials, and to clarify or add emphasis. See 614.3, 614.4, 616.3, and 616.5 in *Write Source*.

> **Add** commas where they are needed below. Write the rule that applies in each case.

1. The plane plunged from 18,000 feet to 16,000 feet in less than five seconds.

Rule: *Commas separate numerals in large numbers in order to distinguish*

hundreds, thousands, millions, and so forth.

2. What happened happened without warning.

Rule: _____

3. The pilot heard the engine cough and then a terrible silence.

Rule: _____

4. The pilot as a matter of fact would have preferred even the sound of an ailing engine to the ominous quiet.

Rule: _____

_____

5. "This is definitely not what John Henry Sr. had in mind when he suggested that his little boy take up flying as a hobby," thought the pilot wryly.

Rule: _____

6. The altimeter continued to drop: 15300, 15000, 14000, . . . and an alarm began to sound.

Rule: _____

_____

7. The alarm grew louder by the second until finally it stopped abruptly. (I had reached over and turned off my alarm clock.)

Rule: _____

_____

Review: Commas 2

> **Add** commas where they are needed below. Write the rule that applies in each case.

1. Did you know, Joy, that a whale's heart beats about nine times a minute?

Rule: _Commas set off nouns of direct address._

2. Hey please turn the music down! I'm trying to get some sleep!

Rule: _____

3. "The human body contains 206 bones" explained Mr. Brown our biology teacher "with about 50 of them in the feet."

Rule: _____

Rule: _____

4. Although you may not believe it the adult human body has 100000 miles of blood vessels.

Rule: _____

Rule: _____

5. James Rudan D.D.S. will be extracting all of my wisdom teeth.

Rule: _____

6. It is the female bee not the male that does all the work in and around the hive.

Rule: _____

7. Sari who is planning to major in psychology has already enrolled at the University of Maryland.

Rule: _____

8. Her address will be 822 Tenth Street Apartment D Baltimore MD 00823.

Rule: _____

Review: Semicolons & Colons

> **Insert** colons or semicolons where they are needed in the following paragraphs.

1   One brilliant physicist stands above all others of our time Stephen

2   Hawking. His writings have greatly advanced our understanding of the

3   universe. Dr. Hawking explains sophisticated theories in language the

4   average person can understand in other words, he has brought the outer

5   limits of space "down to earth."

6   Stephen Hawking has a disabling disease amyotrophic lateral sclerosis

7   (ALS). This disease gradually destroys the nerves and muscles needed for

8   moving. In 1962, when he was only 20 years old, doctors told Hawking

9   that he would probably die before he earned his Ph.D. however, their

10   patient, who is one of today's best-known scientists, proved them wrong.

11   Dr. Hawking is most famous for his study of black holes. These

12   phenomena—possibly formed when a star burns itself out and collapses—

13   are areas in which gravity is extremely strong anything pulled into the

14   black hole cannot get out. (Even time stops!)

15   You can learn more about this subject in Hawking's *A Brief History*

16   *of Time: From the Big Bang to Black Holes*. The book is remarkable,

17   especially when you consider this It was written by a man who speaks

18   with difficulty and cannot move his arms and hands. 33

Hyphens

Turn to the rules for hyphens at 624.1–626.5 in *Write Source*. When using rule 624.3 to form a compound adjective, check a dictionary. You may find your word spelled without a hyphen, as in *bighearted*.

> **Add** hyphens where they are needed in the sentences below.

1. Did you end up writing a four-, five-, or six-page essay?

2. My mother doesn't like my brother's easy going attitude.

3. Was that a velvet lined cloak that Sir Raleigh spread in the mud?

4. He is supposed to do two thirds of the chores.

5. Our town is full of one way streets, and my sister in law gets lost.

6. My great grandfather will be 99 next month.

7. He is a soft spoken person.

8. Is that an R rated movie?

9. The 65 year old woman wore a purple T shirt.

10. Do those boards come in 8, 10, and 12 foot lengths?

11. Is that really a two carat diamond?

12. In 1952, Vincent Massey became the first Canadian born governor general.

13. The flag of Canada features an eleven point red maple leaf.

14. The Civil War (1861 1865) divided Americans on a number of issues.

15. The lawyer knew that what she did would have far reaching consequences.

16. However, she mistakenly considered herself all powerful.

17. I would like to know all of my relatives, but I'll have to settle for knowing my great grandmother, my great aunt, and my two cousins.

18. I love those crescent shaped Christmas cookies.

Extend: Go back to the first five sentences above and write the number of the rule in *Write Source* that shows why you added each hyphen.

Dashes

Dashes are used to indicate a sudden break in the flow of a sentence, to emphasize an idea, or to set off words that explain or clarify something. Turn to 640.1–640.5 in *Write Source*.

> **Read** the following sentences by the Wyoming writer Gretel Ehrlich, who writes about the side of cowboys most people don't know. Study her use of dashes and answer the questions that follow.

1. More often than not, circumstances—like the colt he's riding or an unexpected blizzard—are overpowering him.
2. In a rancher's world, courage has less to do with facing danger than with acting spontaneously—usually on behalf of an animal or another rider.
3. What we've interpreted as toughness—weathered skin, calloused hands, a squint in the eye, and a growl in the voice—only masks the tenderness inside.
4. So many of the men who came to the West were Southerners—men looking for work and a new life after the Civil War—that chivalrousness and strict codes of honor were soon thought of as western traits.

What kinds of material do the dashes set off? _____

_____

_____

What would be the effect on these sentences if all the material between the

dashes were dropped out? _____

_____

_____

In most of these sentences, would commas work as well as dashes? Explain why

or why not. _____

_____

_____

_____

Extend: From what you have observed about dashes by reading Ehrlich's sentences and by looking at the data in your textbook, write a paragraph explaining when and how and why to use dashes. In your paragraph, make sure that at least three of your sentences use dashes—in other words, practice what you preach.

Review: Hyphens & Dashes

> **Put** hyphens and dashes where they are needed in the following passage.

1   If it weren't for my great-great great grandfather, I would have

2   finished my homework well, I might have finished it. Anyway, the whole

3   episode started with my sister and me playing hide and seek in the park

4   near our high rise apartment. Sometimes let's just say on those evenings

5   when my patience hasn't been used up I pretend that I don't know where

6   she is. But last night was different she didn't hide. She stood in front of

7   the Civil War Monument, pointing at it.

8   "Look," she said. I did and saw the name Patrick Flannery. "It's

9   Grandpa," she added.

10   "It can't be Grandpa," I replied. "He's eighty seven. That's too young

11   to have been in the Civil War." I pointed to a plaque that showed the

12   dates of the war: 1861 1865.

13   "You're wrong!" she said. "That's Grandpa."

14   Obviously, she's a one of a kind sister. She decided to go ask Mom.

15   The elevator crawled. We watched floor numbers five, six, seven, . . .

16   My sister took advantage of the slow moving elevator and told everyone

17   inside that our grandfather was a hero a *Civil War* hero. She sounded

18   so proud.

19   When we got home, Mom said, "Call Grandpa."

20   Grandpa asked us to come over. When we arrived, he had spread out

21   a table full of things. It turned out that Patrick Flannery was Grandpa's

22   great grandfather. And surprise, surprise he was a Civil War hero!

Apostrophes in Contractions & Plurals

An apostrophe is used to show where letters have been omitted in contractions (as in *don't*). An apostrophe is also used to form the plural of a letter, a number, a sign, or a word discussed as a word. Turn to 628.1 and 630.4 in *Write Source* for examples and additional rules.

> **Insert** apostrophes where they are needed in the sentences below.

1. Theres nothing I like better than telling someone to mind their ps and qs!

2. "Youre really going to appreciate the sound quality on that new television youve got there," the salesperson assured us.

3. How many *ss* does the word *Mississippi* have?

4. I wouldnt have noticed anything was wrong if you hadnt spoken up.

5. Can you see whats holding everything up?

6. We couldnt walk around the lake because the bridge over the canal hadnt been repaired yet.

7. I didnt know you could use so many *had*s in one sentence!

8. Oh, Im great! Howve you been? Hows your brother?

9. Were going to study for the exam together so we can both get As.

10. Once a comb has lost its teeth, its no longer useful.

11. I havent been able to sleep; I keep thinking about what couldve happened to my friends and me if wed hit that truck.

12. My interviewer asked how many As and Bs I had on my last report card.

13. Are you a member of the class of 11?

14. "I'm just hangin out," Joey said.

15. Do you know the dos and donts of good writing?

Extend: Do you know the difference between *its* and *it's, who's* and *whose, your* and *you're*? Write three sentences using one of these easily confused pairs in each sentence. Exchange papers with a classmate. Correct each other's work if necessary. Turn to pages 688 and 696 in *Write Source* for assistance.

Apostrophes to Form Possessives 1

The possessive form of a singular noun is usually created by adding an apostrophe and an *s*. The possessive form of a plural that ends in *s* is usually formed by adding an apostrophe at the end (*fire-eaters'*). If a plural noun does not end in *s* (*children*), the possessive is usually formed by adding an apostrophe and an *s* (*children's*). Turn to 628.2–628.3 in *Write Source*.

Add apostrophes and *s's* where they are needed in the sentences below.

1. You'll never figure out which poster is Mary ^{'s}.

2. My brother cereal bowl is still sitting on the table.

3. Where did all of the Smiths mail and packages go?

4. I hadn't even considered a lawyer involvement.

5. Monkeys tails are strong.

6. I'll never understand why Steve sister wants one of those cars.

7. Our womens basketball team is as popular as the mens team.

8. Do you know what Portugal greatest natural resource is?

9. Two months pay won't cover the bill.

10. My stepmother brother still lives in upstate New York.

11. Some Greek gods temples were built on islands in the Aegean Sea.

12. Have you ever seen anything as funny-looking as Mr. and Mrs. Jones dog?

13. He is a wolf in sheeps clothing.

Write sentences using both the singular and plural possessive form of these two words: *candle* and *child*.

_____

_____

_____

_____

Apostrophes to Form Possessives 2

The possessive form of a singular noun is usually created by adding an apostrophe and an *s*. Turn to 628.2 in *Write Source*. The possessive form of a plural that ends in *s* is usually formed by adding an apostrophe at the end (*fire-eaters'*). If a plural noun does not end in *s* (*children*), the possessive is usually formed by adding an apostrophe and an *s* (*children's*). Turn to 628.3 in *Write Source*.

> **Add** apostrophes and *s's* where they are needed in the sentences below.

1. Both dogs' toys have been gnawed into unidentifiable chunks of plastic.

2. My teacher instructions were clear and concise, but we didn't have time to finish the project.

3. Our bosses pictures hang on the wall.

4. Chaz backpack was destroyed in the same blaze that razed the public library.

5. Have you seen the triplets matching outfits?

6. Everyone in town knew that the sheriff badge was stainless steel.

7. How many of the couples tickets have we collected so far?

8. Tess story was the best.

9. Please put this in the childrens room.

10. Fergus story was the most likeable.

11. The Coen brothers movies are famous.

12. The countries flags flew over their fallen soldiers graves.

> **Write** sentences using both the singular and plural possessive form for these two words: *pizza* and *Miller* (a family's surname).

_____

_____

_____

Apostrophes to Form Possessives 3

When possession is shared by more than one noun, use the possessive form for the last noun in the series (*Lonny and Sarah's house*). To form the possessive of a compound noun or of a two- or three-word indefinite pronoun, add an apostrophe and *s* to the last word (the *secretary of state's* speech, *somebody else's* truck). Turn to 630.1–630.2 in *Write Source* for more information.

> **Write** your own sentences using possessives as suggested.

1. Sarah, Laurie, and Marci own a large tent.

Sarah, Laurie, and Marci's tent is large.

2. Show that everyone but you has sore eyes.

_____

3. Emma and Hannah own a doghouse that has a front porch.

_____

4. Show that nobody but you has a flashlight that works.

_____

5. Show that there was a meeting this morning about the athletic budget.

_____

6. Mom and Dad share possession of a car that has a sunroof.

_____

7. Show that Opal and Jed own a new computer that operates their security system.

_____

8. Show that Suze's mother-in-law owns a very valuable antique ring.

_____

9. Show that someone (use *someone* as an indefinite pronoun) possesses a lawn mower that needs a muffler.

_____

Review: Apostrophes

> **Write** the correct form of each word that appears in italics in the blank provided. (Add apostrophes and s's where they are needed.)

1. Pearl _____*Buck's*_____ *(Buck)* Nobel Prize for literature was awarded to her in 1938.

2. The _____ *(boss)* office had a window and an air conditioner, but _____ *(Dennis)* office _____ *(didnt)* even have a window.

3. The carpeting is being replaced in the _____ *(programmers)* offices.

4. Esther, Jamie, and Ed hurried into the _____ *(children)* room.

5. The department _____ *(store)* Santa Claus was tired.

6. He felt he had really earned this _____ *(day)* wage.

7. _____ *(Somebody else)* lap would have to hold the kiddies tomorrow.

8. He said, "I _____ *(dont)* think _____ *(Ill)* come to work for a week! _____ *(Santa)* going to rest."

9. Mrs. Sloan told us to watch our _____ *(p)* and _____ *(q)* and always be polite to our parents and our _____ *(parents)* friends.

10. Her _____ *(great-grandmother)* antiques were sold at auction today.

11. Will _____ *(Black, Christer, and Tott)* law firm help with that deposition?

Quotation Marks with Dialogue

Quotation marks are used in written dialogue, enclosing a speaker's exact words. Turn to 632.1 and 632.2 in *Write Source*. Remember, a new paragraph shows a change of speaker.

> **Insert** the missing quotation marks and commas in the quotations that follow. Use the symbol ¶ to show where a new paragraph should begin.

1. "What in the world are you doing here?" she asked, regarding her disheveled sister with well-bred surprise. ¶ "Gathering leaves," meekly answered Jo.

—Louisa May Alcott, *Little Women*

2. It's the children said Mrs. Parsons, casting a half-apprehensive glance at the door. They haven't been out today.

—George Orwell, *1984*

3. He said Don't tell anyone our secret. I nodded my head with all the sobriety I could muster, although I wanted to scream to the world We have a secret!

—Jane Hamilton, *The Book of Ruth*

4. Suddenly Sir Kay reined in his horse in dismay. My sword! he cried. I left my sword where we lodged last night!

—retold by Emma G. Sterne and Barbara Lindsay, *King Arthur and the Knights of the Round Table*

5. Stop! said the man. Good day, said Theseus. Now, listen, stranger, everyone who passes this way washes my feet. That's the toll. Any questions?

—retold by Bernard Evslin, *Theseus*

6. How long can you hold him? asks Bill. I'm not as strong as I used to be, says old Dorset, but I think I can promise you ten minutes.

—O. Henry, *The Ransom of Red Chief*

Extend: Collect three to five samples of dialogue from books, newspapers, and magazines. Study the examples with a classmate and answer these questions: (1) When do writers use dialogue? (2) Does the usage of dialogue differ between nonfiction and fiction? (3) What purposes does dialogue have?

Quotation Marks with Direct Quotations

Quotation marks enclose a direct quotation (the exact words of a speaker). See 632.1 in *Write Source*.

> **Add** quotation marks to the direct quotations below. If a quotation is indirect, rewrite the sentence to make the quotation direct.

1. Mary says that we should test our smoke alarms to make sure they work.

Mary said, "We should test our smoke alarms to make sure

they work."

2. The state of Vermont, the travel agent said, is breathtaking in October.

_____

_____

3. If you are interested in trying out for the school play, she reminded the students, pick up a copy of the script on your way out.

_____

_____

4. The vet explained that dogs and cats raised in the same household usually get along.

_____

_____

5. I don't want to bother you, Pete whispered, but could I borrow a pencil?

_____

_____

6. When Emily got a flat tire, she told her father she could fix it herself.

_____

_____

Extend: Write and punctuate a conversation between you and another person, using direct quotations.

Italics (Underlining) & Quotation Marks

Some titles and special words appear in quotation marks, while others appear in italics (or are underlined). Review the rules at on page 636 in *Write Source*.

> **Place** quotation marks around or underline (to indicate italics) the titles or special words below that require either quotation marks or italics.

1. "Where Are You Going, Where Have You Been?" (short story)

2. Introduction to French Literature (book)

3. Paris's Left Bank (magazine article)

4. Laurie Makes Mischief and Jo Makes Peace (chapter title)

5. By the Skin of Our Teeth (full-length play)

6. Sleep Better, Starting Tonight (magazine article)

7. 7th Heaven (TV program)

8. Legion of Merit (video)

9. How to Choose a College (pamphlet)

10. Room at the Top of the World (song)

11. Little Miss Muffet (nursery rhyme)

12. Robert E. Lee's One Mistake (lecture)

13. A Prairie Home Companion (radio program)

14. Air Force One (specific name of an airplane)

15. Hartford's Free Press (newspaper)

16. Annabel Lee (poem)

17. King Kong (film)

18. lemmus (scientific classification of lemming)

19. Chicago Tribune (newspaper)

20. Pride and Prejudice (book)

21. The Hollow Men (poem)

22. Old Ironsides (ship)

23. The Rising (CD)

24. Macbeth (full-length play)

25. McCall's (magazine)

26. The Gift (short story)

27. bien vu (foreign words)

28. Madame Butterfly (opera)

29. Spruce Goose (specific name of an airplane)

30. The Nobel Prize Winners (lecture)

Review: Quotation Marks & Italics (Underlining)

> **Add** quotation marks and italics where they are needed in the sentences below. (Use underlining to indicate italics.)

1. "You've never read <u>Moby Dick</u>! the teacher exclaimed. "Well, to be honest," he said, "neither have I."

2. My brother told me that he went to a lecture called Physics for Poets.

3. I really hope she casts me in the role of Nora in the three-act play A Doll's House, Michelle sighed.

4. For our group presentation, you are responsible for the chapter entitled Wind and Water Energy, and I'll take the next chapter, Nuclear Energy.

5. Did you know that the Wizard of Oz is a film that is based on a book?

6. At my cousin's wedding, my uncle got up and danced when the song Blue Suede Shoes was played.

7. Sammi found this quotation to support her thesis statement: Most people who use the Internet do so because they have a desire for information, they understand how to use a computer, and they have access to the Internet.

8. Who has a favorite poem? our English teacher, Ms. Amontu, asked.

9. Raymond Healy's hand shot into the air like a missile. I love The Base Stealer, he said.

10. Really? Can you quote it? asked Ms. Amontu.

11. Sure. He began, Poised between going on and back, pulled / Both ways taut like a tightrope-walker, / Fingertips pointing the opposites, / Now bouncing tiptoe like a dropped ball.

12. Great! cried Ms. Amontu laughing. I think everyone should have a favorite poem and be able to recite it.

Punctuation for Research Papers 1

This exercise is designed to help you become more familiar with the punctuation marks often needed in research papers.

> **Add** punctuation in the following sentences after checking the section in *Write Source* that is indicated in parentheses. Answer the questions on the lines provided.

1. Edgar Allan Poe was born to David Poe, Jr., and Elizabeth Poe. (644.4)

2. To Poe, poetry was more than a job "With me, poetry has been not a purpose but a passion." (620.4)

3. One example of Poe's use of Greek references is found in his poem To Helen. Poe writes, Helen, thy beauty is to me / Like those Nicéan barks of yore. (632.1 and 634.3)

4. The poem also includes consonance in some lines "The weary, way-worn wanderer bore To his own native shore." (620.4 and 638.4)

5. Poe also uses consonance in his poem The Raven. For example, consider these lines "Followed fast and followed faster till his [the raven's] songs one burden bore." (634.3 and 620.4)

Why are brackets used? (page 644) _____

_____

6. Poe also uses internal rhyme in his poetry when he says "Though thy crest be shorn and shaven, thou, I said, art sure no craven." (616.1)

7. He uses many techniques: "Poe's use of allusion, analogy, parallelism, rhyme, and rythm *sic* is amazing." (644.2)

8. In a magazine article, The Philosophy of Composition, published in Graham's Magazine in April 1846, Poe writes about the "tones" of beauty and sadness. (634.3 and 636.2)

9. Poe's view of tone is found in his statement "All experience has shown that this tone is one of sadness. . . . Melancholy is thus the most legitimate of all the poetical tones."

Why is an ellipsis used? (page 642) _____

_____

Punctuation for Research Papers 2

Research papers often include data and information from books, magazines, newspapers, computer files, and interviews. Turn to the following sections in *Write Source* to review the punctuation marks that are often needed when you include data in a research paper: 642.1–642.2 (ellipsis), 616.1 (comma), 620.5 (colon), 644.1–644.3 (brackets), and 632.1–632.3 (quotation marks) as well as pages 450–451 (punctuation for electronic sources).

> **Read** the following paragraphs and focus on the punctuation that comes just before the number in parentheses. Then fill in the blank at the bottom of the page with the number of the rule that explains why each punctuation mark has been used.

"The Masque of the Red Death," (1) one of Edgar Allan Poe's most famous short stories, is filled with symbolism. Both colors and numbers are symbols. According to Martha Womack, who created the Web site Precisely Poe, (2) "In this story, the plague takes the unusual form of a red death . . . (3) so that blood, the very substance of life, now becomes the mark of death." (4) Poe writes, (5) "But first let me tell of the rooms . . . (6) There were seven." (7) Womack reminds the reader of the historical significance of seven: (8) "The history of the world was thought to consist of seven ages, just as an individual's life had seven stages. The ancient world had seven wonders; universities divided learning into seven subjects; there were seven deadly sins [pride, avarice, etc.] (9) with seven corresponding virtues [humility, generosity, etc.]."

Dr. Jorge Parkman, my instructor and a literary critic, said, "The interpretation of symbolism can show an individual's opinion and bias. Be scholarly—very scholarly—when interpreting symbols [in literature] (10)." (11)

1. _640.1_   4. _____   7. _____   10. _____

2. _____   5. _____   8. _____   11. _____

3. _____   6. _____   9. _____

Punctuation for Research Papers 3

The type of punctuation you use with quoted material will depend on how long or short the quotation is. Turn to page 424 in *Write Source*.

> **Write** answers for the following questions.

1. How many lines does a short quotation have? *four or less* _____

2. How should a short quotation be incorporated into a research paper? _____

_____

3. What punctuation is used to set off a short quotation? _____

4. How many lines does a long quotation have? _____

5. How should a long quotation be incorporated into a research paper? _____

_____

_____

6. How should the second paragraph of a long quotation be included? _____

_____

7. Are quotation marks used with long quotations? _____

_____

8. How many lines does a short poetic quotation have? _____

9. How should a short poetic quotation be incorporated into a research paper? ____

_____

_____

10. What punctuation mark shows where a line of poetry ends? _____

11. How should poetic quotations of four lines or more be incorporated into a paper?

_____

12. What punctuation mark shows that you have left out part of a quotation?

_____

MLA Style

Turn to pages 429–436 in *Write Source*.

> **Write** a correct MLA works-cited entry for each of the sources described below.

1. An article by Matthew Battles in *Harper's* magazine entitled "Lost in the Stacks: The Decline and Fall of the Universal Library." The article appeared in January 2000 and was printed on pages 36–39.

Battles, Matthew. "Lost in the Stacks: The Decline and Fall of the Universal

Library." Harper's Jan. 2000: 36–39. Print.

2. A book entitled *Mexicanos: A History of Mexicans in the United States* by Manuel G. Gonzales. It was published in Bloomington, Indiana, by Indiana University Press in 1999.

_____

_____

_____

3. An article entitled "The Day We Found George Mallory" that appeared on the BBC Web site in 2000. The article was written by Peter Firstbrook. It was retrieved on February 24, 2005, from the World Wide Web at this address: http://www.bbc.co.uk.

_____

_____

_____

4. A film entitled *Madiba: The Life and Times of Nelson Mandela*. It was directed and produced by Robert Benger in 2004.

_____

_____

_____

5. An article entitled "Catherine the Great" in *The New Encyclopaedia Britannica* published in 2005.

_____

APA Style

Turn to pages 437–438 in *Write Source*.

> **Write** a correct APA reference entry for each of the sources described below.

1. A book called *America's First Ladies: Their Lives and Their Legacies*. It was written by Lewis L. Gould and published by Routledge in New York in 2001.

Gould, L. L. (2001). America's first ladies: Their lives and their legacies.

New York: Routledge.

2. An article entitled "Coyote and Wolf Habitat Use in Northwestern Montana" that appeared in the magazine *Northwest Science*. It was written by Wendy M. Arjo and Daniel H. Pletscher and published in 2004, volume 78, on pages 24–32.

_____

_____

_____

3. A newspaper article entitled "Global Death Rates Drop for Children 5 or Younger" that appeared in the newspaper *The New York Times* on May 23, 2010. It was written by Denise Grady and appeared on page 4 of section A.

_____

_____

_____

4. A collection of rare books and pamphlets called *Votes for Women: Selections from the National American Woman Suffrage Association Collection, 1848–1921* located on the Library of Congress Web site. The page is dated October 19, 1998, and it was retrieved on March 18, 2005. The Web address for the page is http://www.memory.loc.gov/ammem/naw/nawshome.html.

_____

_____

_____

_____

Punctuation to Create Emphasis

Punctuation can be used to emphasize a particular word or phrase in a sentence. Dashes and colons and, of course, exclamation points often serve this purpose. Occasionally, commas are also used to emphasize a word or a phrase. Turn to 640.5 (dashes), 620.3 (colons), 605.4 (exclamation points), and 616.5 (commas) in *Write Source*.

> **Study** the sentences below. Circle the punctuation marks that are used to create emphasis and underline the part of the sentence that is emphasized. Then use each sentence as a model for a sentence of your own.

1. "He saw only dreams and memories, and heard music." (from "Home" by Langston Hughes)

The children played with pebbles and twigs, and made fun.

2. "He's been a prisoner here longer than anyone else: thirty-three years." (from *Life Sentences* by Wilbert Rideau)

_____

3. "He's the kind of man who picks his friends—to pieces." (Mae West)

_____

4. "I could smell Mama, crisp and starched, plumping my pillow . . . ." (from *A Day No Pigs Would Die* by Robert Newton Peck)

_____

5. She was on tiptoe, stretching for an orange, when they heard, "HEY YOU!"

_____

_____

Note: What additional technique is used to create emphasis in this sentence?

_____

6. "Without the hatchet he had nothing—no fire, no tools, no weapons." (from *Hatchet* by Gary Paulson)

_____

_____

Note: What additional technique is used to create emphasis in this sentence?

_____

Brackets & Parentheses

Brackets enclose words that you add to a direct quotation. Turn to 644.1–644.3 in your *Write Source*. Parentheses (which should be used sparingly) enclose explanatory or added material. Turn to 638.1–638.2 in *Write Source*.

> **Insert** missing words and add sic where appropriate below, using brackets. The material is quoted directly from the 1805 journals of Lewis and Clark.

1. *Clark, July 17:* The yellow currents [sic] [are] now ripe and the fussey [sic] red chokecherries are getting ripe.

2. I climbed a spur of the mountains, which I found to be high and dificult of axcess.

3. *Lewis, July 18:* Previous to our departure saw a large herd of bighorn on the high clift opposite us.

4. *Clark, July 18:* I passed over a mountain on an Indian rode, and we camped on a small run of clear cold water. Musquitors are very troublesome.

> **Add** parentheses below to enclose explanatory material. Also add parentheses to any asides that interrupt the flow of a sentence.

1. Many of the spellings (or rather, the *mis*spellings) that Lewis and Clark used were also wrong in 1805.

2. The misspellings *fussey* for *fuzzy, clift* for *cliff, rode* for *road* confused many readers then and today.

3. Lewis's poor spelling is a surprise, considering his background. Lewis was President Thomas Jefferson's private secretary.

Extend: Write a journal entry of three sentences. Omit several words and misspell some. Exchange papers with a classmate. Use brackets to add any needed words and corrections to your partner's paper.

Pretest: Capitalization

> **Cross** out the lowercase letter and write the capital letter above it in each word that should be capitalized in the following sentences.

1. In *L̶*atin american history 101, one of our school's classes for juniors, we saw a movie about costa rica.

2. It's a tiny central american country, smaller than the state of west virginia.

3. costa rica is bordered by nicaragua on the north, the caribbean sea on the east, panama on the south, and the pacific ocean on the west.

4. Its capital, san jose, has approximately 335,000 people.

5. Like most central american countries, costa rica was a spanish colony until it won its independence in 1821.

6. Every year costa rica celebrates its independence from spain on september 18; the United States celebrates its independence from britain on july 4.

7. costa rica is one of the few countries in central or south america that doesn't have a standing army.

8. Just about everyone (myself included) has a hard time imagining a country without a military.

9. In 1987, president oscar arias sanchez won the nobel peace prize for his role in trying to bring peace to the region.

10. Tourists like this caribbean paradise because it has miles and miles of incredible beaches on both the east and west sides of the country.

11. *A guide to the birds of costa rica,* by f. gary stiles, tells about the toucans, parrots, and other birds that live in the rain forests in costa rica.

12. Sometimes people who visit these rain forests experience culture shock when they later visit the capital city of san jose and see neon-sign advertisements for american, european, and japanese tourists.

13. My uncle made a u-turn in his life when he moved to costa rica last spring.

14. This is what uncle charley wrote to my dad: "what I love about my home here is that there is no telephone, no computer, or no tv."

15. Sounds like my uncle (who has a ph.d. in engineering) got sick of corporate america.

16. On dad's nightstand, i saw a copy of a book called *costa rica: the last country the gods made.*

17. I hope he is not thinking of moving our family there—at least not before I graduate.

18. I think dad would have a hard time watching birds rather than the green bay packers on weekends.

Capitalize the following words that need capitalization.

1. spring, monday

2. uncle zeke, my uncle

3. a japanese tea, the tearoom

4. ohio, ireland

5. the renaissance

6. the nineteenth century

7. october, middle ages

8. north of boston, turn north

9. mayor cummings, the mayor

10. fbi, a federal agency

11. *the sun also rises*

12. "the diary of a madman"

13. my english class, my math class

14. the democratic party, a political party

Capitalization 1

Turn to pages 648–652 in *Write Source* for rules on capitalization.

> **Underline** any word below that is capitalized incorrectly (or not capitalized when it should be).

1. My <u>Mother</u> asked, "<u>when</u> are you leaving?"

2. We are driving North to Canada this Spring.

3. I love the West. The midwest is too flat for my taste.

4. During those long hours in the car (We'll drive 12 hours the first day), we can listen to Books on Tape.

5. I like listening to the british readers better than the American ones.

6. The laotian boy has learned to speak english very well.

7. The group from europe speaks a number of languages: german, spanish, and french.

8. Most italian people are catholic, but some are buddhist.

9. In the south, grits is a popular dish. (grits is a term for ground corn.)

10. In a 1955 Interview, John Mason Brown had this to say about tv: "some television programs are so much chewing gum for the eyes."

11. When auntie Anne came to visit, she read poems to us.

12. I liked her readings, especially the poems by robert frost.

13. Grandpa loves to dig up the garden by hand before planting his Yukon Gold Potatoes.

14. Yes, this Summer my girl scout troop will travel to nova scotia.

15. I saw signs in chicago that showed how to follow the original route 66 through the city.

Capitalization 2

Turn to pages 648–652 in *Write Source* for capitalization rules.

> **Underline** any word below that is capitalized incorrectly (or not capitalized when it should be).

1. The soundtrack to <u>South Pacific</u> stayed on the charts for 115 weeks..

2. The North Cape vikings basketball uniform is black and purple.

3. Nini Purimi, ph.d, was awarded the top prize for her thesis, "The Blending of Culture In The Modern Americas."

4. John travolta, became a star after he appeared in the movie *Saturday night fever*.

5. Over the thanksgiving holiday last Fall, we traveled through four States on interstate 94.

6. Laura works at the v.f.w. post, where the local Veterans hold their New Year's eve parties.

7. The Blackmailer demanded money for his silence regarding the Boston tea party.

8. The Arlington high school forensics club won the Statewide competition.

9. The latino populations in some U.S. Cities celebrate cinco de mayo, a Mexican Holiday.

10. Mayor John Jennson was surprised by a Labor day visit from Anna Lopez, the Governor.

11. Will the festival be on the last saturday in may or right before Mother's day?

12. Burlington high school has a radio station, wbsd.

Capitalization 3

Turn to pages 648–652 in *Write Source* for capitalization rules.

> **Underline** any word below that is capitalized incorrectly (or not capitalized when it should be).

1. Nouns that refer to the <u>supreme</u> <u>being</u> are capitalized.

2. In greek mythology, Hercules was the son of Zeus, the King of the greek gods.

3. I am enrolled in a History course about the bible; it's called "History as Portrayed in The Bible."

4. When Rasheed was a Sophomore, a freshman invited him to the Sadie Hawkins dance.

5. "Ask aunt Clara if she'd like to join us," dad said. "she might have fun."

6. "Praise the lord!" my Mom exclaimed.

7. When he was President of the club, Frank suggested some great Projects.

8. Nadia is taking trigonometry 200 this semester, since she took her first Trigonometry course last year.

9. In the American southwest, native American art is very popular.

10. The owner of the Milwaukee bucks (an nba basketball team) is senator Herb Kohl, a democrat from Wisconsin.

11. Emmy, who lives in anchorage, Alaska, has her own home page on the web; she is also one of the organizers for the Dave Matthews fan club.

12. Will professor Nintri be teaching History 201 this Semester?

13. All the Juniors will be required to take either sociology or spanish.

Extend: Write five sentences that illustrate some of the capitalization rules on pages 648–652 in your textbook. Choose rules that gave you trouble in this exercise.

Review: Capitalization

> **Underline** any word below that is capitalized incorrectly (or not capitalized when it should be).

1. <u>most</u> <u>american</u> workers get <u>labor</u> <u>day</u> off.

2. The Mayor is going to speak every Tuesday in August.

3. Eighty-fourth Avenue is on the East side of town.

4. Isn't your Mother from the East?

5. I heard mom calling for you, Dad.

6. I've always liked History Courses.

7. Are you taking history 201 next Fall?

8. Castles were quite common in the Middle ages.

9. the battle of Bunker Hill claimed many lives.

10. an Alaskan eskimo, a Canadian pilot, and a catholic priest went fishing.

11. Have you read T. S. Eliot's "the Wasteland"?

12. Ronald Reagan, once a democrat, became a republican.

13. The State Park on highway 13 East of town was opened last summer.

14. Go north on Old Summit road.

15. My uncle Marc has worked for NASA since the Winter of '99.

16. My uncle went to the rose bowl and the super bowl.

17. Does lake michigan have car-ferry service?

18. A scenic River like the Colorado attracts many Foreign visitors.

19. let me introduce senator Bob Madsen.

20. Hawaii, the aloha state, is in the middle of the Pacific ocean.

Numbers 1

Become familiar with some basic guidelines for using numbers so that you know when to write numbers as numerals and when to write numbers as words. Turn to page 658 in *Write Source* for more information.

> **Write** the rule number that each statement below demonstrates. Then give a brief explanation of each rule. (*Note:* All numbers are used correctly in the following sentences.)

658.1 **1.** Teresa received four gifts for her birthday. *Numbers from one to nine are usually written as words.*

_____ **2.** Two of her gifts were from her family. _____

_____ **3.** It was a pleasant 72° F in Pittsburgh today. _____

_____ **4.** My brother gets up at 4:00 A.M. to deliver newspapers. _____

_____ **5.** I get paid $5.74 per hour. _____

_____ **6.** Sully found twenty dollars. _____

_____ **7.** I weighed 8 lbs. 3 oz. when I was born. _____

_____ **8.** About 93 percent of our class will go on to school. _____

_____ **9.** The graphic arts department made fifteen 10-foot banners. _____

Numbers 2

There are specific rules about the use of numbers in formal writing. Turn to page 658 in *Write Source*.

> **Write** the correct form (numeral or word) above the underlined numbers below. If the form is already correct, write C above it.

1. *five*
   The 5 basins of the Great Lakes combine to form a single watershed with 1 *one*

   common outlet to the ocean.

2. Lake Superior is the largest of the Great Lakes, with an area of 31,820 square

   miles; Lake Ontario is the smallest, with an area of just over seventy-five

   hundred square miles.

3. Lake Superior is also the coldest of the 5 lakes; its average water temperature

   is 40° F.

4. The Great Lakes contain eighteen percent of the world's fresh surface water.

5. The total volume of the lakes is more than six quadrillion gallons.

6. Spread evenly over the continental United States, the water would be about

   9 and a half feet deep.

7. The lobes of Lakes Michigan and Huron are at the same elevation and are

   connected by the one hundred twenty-foot-deep Mackinac Strait.

8. Mackinac Strait is not a river that separates the lakes; instead, it is a three-

   point-six- to five-mile narrowing of the lakes.

9. You may want to take 2 300-mile trips instead of one six-hundred-mile cruise.

10. If you left at six a.m. in a boat cruising at 40 mph, you wouldn't get to the other

    end of the lake until 9 o'clock at night.

Extend: Write four or five sentences about traveling. Include information about distance, time, and money, using the correct form for the numbers in your sentences.

Abbreviations

Abbreviations, acronyms, and initialisms are used to shorten a word or a phrase. Turn to pages 660–662 in *Write Source* for more information.

Spell out the following abbreviations.

1. PTA *Parent-Teachers Association*
2. Sr. _____
3. m _____
4. lat. _____
5. inc. _____

6. PIN _____
7. Que. (or) QC _____
8. Blvd. _____
9. B.C.E. _____
10. Hon. _____

Abbreviate the following words.

1. Connecticut *Conn. (or) CT*
2. Avenue _____
3. deceased _____
4. example _____
5. portable document format _____

6. Apartment _____
7. standard time _____
8. ultra high frequency _____
9. weekly _____
10. North _____

List five acronyms and five initialisms that you might use in your own writing.

Acronyms	Initialisms
1. _____	1. _____
2. _____	2. _____
3. _____	3. _____
4. _____	4. _____
5. _____	5. _____

Review: Numbers & Abbreviations

> **Circle** the correct choices. (Remember that in formal writing, most words are spelled out, with the exception of a few acceptable abbreviations.)

1. We pulled up to *(thirteen,* **13***)* Donner *(***Street,** *St.)* at *(four,* **4:00***)* **p.m.,** *post meridiem)* on Sunday afternoon.

2. *(Dr., Doctor)* Julio Mendez, *(Junior, Jr.)*, greeted us at the *(Wisconsin, WI)* *(Department, Dept.)* of Health and gave us the *(HIV, human immunodeficiency virus)* brochures to distribute.

3. The package was addressed to *(Mr., Mister)* Carter, at Mercy Hospital on Gammon *(Avenue, Ave.)*, and we needed to deliver it before *(nine, 9:00)* *(a.m., ante meridiem)* the next day.

4. The public garden was *(one hundred ten, 110)* feet wide on the *(NE, northeast)* side of the *(BBB, Better Business Bureau)* building.

5. Our teacher gave us an *(example, ex.)* of an effective *(bibliography, bibliog.)*.

6. The *(pkg., package)* *(without, w/o)* a legible address could not be delivered.

7. *(15, Fifteen)* minutes later, Luke Harrison signed and *(paid, pd.)* for the rental car and we were off.

8. We met *(7, seven)* 10-year-old Little Leaguers from Taiwan at the gas station where we filled up the car with *(8, eight)* *(gallons, gal.)* of gas.

9. *(5, Five)* students forgot to bring their permission slips.

10. Did you make the appointment for *(four p.m, 4:00 p.m.)*?

11. Dad received *(five dollars, $ five)* for his weekly allowance when he was my age.

12. Our group voted *(four to two, 4 to 2)* to go see the *(3 o'clock, three o'clock)* movie.

Pretest: Plurals & Spelling

> **Write** C above each underlined word that is spelled correctly. Write the correction above each underlined word that is misspelled.

1   At one time, the economy of the United <u>States</u> revolved around agriculture.

2   State fairs <u>growed</u> out of that reality. Fairs were a way to celebrate farming,

3   display the <u>lateest</u> farm machinery, and see who raised the best animals and

4   produce. Even though fewer people have any direct <u>connection</u> with farming,

5   there are still 49 state fairs. Only Rhode Island does not have a state fair.

6   Today's state fairs still feature animals and <u>agricultureal</u> products, but

7   they also include carnival rides for <u>childs</u>, car and motorcycle races, music

8   concerts, arcades, dances, and <u>fireworkes</u>. In other words, most state fairs offer

9   <u>somthing</u> for everyone. Some fairs have been <u>struggleing</u> because attendance

10   has <u>dropped</u> even in so-called agricultural states. However, there <u>appears</u> to

11   be new enthusiasm for this longtime tradition. Some places are <u>tring</u> new

12   attractions. For example, in South Dakota a tank full of <u>sharkes</u> is available for

13   those who would like to see what it is like to swim with sharks.

14   Many fairs are doing well. Minnesota has one of the most popular state

15   fairs. Attendance <u>varyes</u> during the <u>week</u> (the last week in August through

16   Labor Day). One of the best days saw 225,249 people munching corn dogs,

17   slurping slushes, eating cheese curds, and enjoying the sights, sounds, and

18   smells of the fair.

19   State fairs are a tradition and part of our <u>nationnal</u> heritage. They recall

20   an <u>earlyer</u> time and life close to the land. At the same time, these fairs <u>revael</u>

21   the changes in agriculture as <u>computors</u> now calculate the best times to plant

22   and harvest.

Write the plurals of the following nouns on the lines provided.

1. chef _chefs_

2. ABC _____

3. sheep _____

4. crisis _____

5. father-in-law _____

6. 5 _____

7. spoonful _____

8. tattoo _____

9. latchkey _____

10. rash _____

11. editor in chief _____

12. party _____

13. veto _____

14. shelf _____

Fill in the blanks or circle the correct spelling. All the information you will need pertains to spelling rules.

1. Write *i* before _____ except after *c*, or when sounded like *a* as in *neighbor* and *weigh*.

2. Using the rule stated above, circle each correctly spelled word:

receive, recieve; reign, riegn; seige, siege; belief, beleif.

3. When a one-syllable word (*mat*) ends in a consonant (*t*) preceded by one vowel (*a*), _____ the final consonant before adding a suffix that begins with a vowel (-*ing*).

4. Using the rule stated above, add the suffix -*ary* to the word *sum*: _____.

5. If a word ends with a silent *e*, _____ the *e* before adding a suffix that begins with a vowel.

6. Using the rule stated above, add *ing* to the following words: make, drive, write.

_____

Plurals 1

An *es* or *s* is added to the end of most singular nouns in order to form the plurals. But nouns ending in *y, o, f,* or *fe* present exceptions to this basic *es* or *s* rule. Turn to page 654 in *Write Source* for more information.

Make the following words plural.

1. horse *horses*
2. radio
3. story
4. holiday
5. potato
6. pass
7. church
8. wife

9. buzz
10. tomato
11. leaf
12. fly
13. patio
14. birch
15. monkey
16. push

Change the following plurals to their singular form.

1. bowls *bowl*
2. rushes
3. tries
4. heroes
5. trios
6. ewes
7. jalopies

8. folios
9. fryers
10. satellites
11. roles
12. roofs
13. cries
14. parties

Extend: Create your own version of the exercise at the top of the page. Think of five new words that form plurals using the rules you've just studied. List the singular forms. Then trade papers with a classmate and complete one another's exercise.

Plurals 2

This exercise focuses on three rules: forming the plurals of words that end in *f* or *fe*; creating the plurals of irregular words; and forming the plurals of compound nouns. Turn to 656.1, 656.2, and 654.6 in *Write Source*.

Write the plural form of each word below.

1. loaf *loaves*
2. belief
3. knife
4. calf
5. half
6. wolf
7. chief
8. cliff

9. thief
10. fife
11. life
12. sniff
13. staff
14. strife
15. puff
16. elf

Change each of the following irregular and compound words to its plural form.

1. die *dice (or) dies*
2. ox
3. mouse
4. goose
5. tooth
6. woman
7. syllabus

8. editor in chief
9. son-in-law
10. aide-de-camp
11. maid-in-waiting
12. secretary-general
13. two-wheeler
14. vertebra

Extend: Create your own version of the exercises at the top of the page. Think of five new words that form plurals using the rules you've just studied. List the singular forms. Then trade papers with a classmate and complete one another's exercise.

Spelling 1

Turn to page 664 in *Write Source* to find spelling rules that will help you with this exercise. Learn the rules and exceptions as you work. (You may also use your dictionary.)

Circle the word that is spelled incorrectly in each pair below. Then write the correct spelling in the blank.

1. (feild,) losing _____*field*_____
2. lonly, shiniest _____
3. useful, robery _____
4. sentries, safty _____
5. peice, puppies _____
6. likly, committed _____
7. behaving, truely _____
8. nieghborhood, plier _____
9. alleys, firey _____
10. finely, ladys _____
11. biege, occurred _____
12. monkies, quitter _____
13. referred, cryed _____
14. dying, joging _____
15. luckily, refered _____
16. receipt, drugist _____
17. management, thier _____
18. nineth, freight _____
19. liesure, mileage _____
20. advertisement, pennys _____

21. mischeif, friend _____
22. living, mudied _____
23. ninteen, ponies _____
24. decieve, fiend _____
25. comeing, chief _____
26. judgment, lovly _____
27. guidance, deisel _____
28. allies, admitance _____
29. flies, arguement _____
30. lovable, hygeine _____
31. desireable, bugged _____
32. sumary, happiness _____
33. baggage, useing _____
34. likness, plugged _____
35. field, valueable _____
36. vein, niether _____
37. conceit, beautyful _____
38. canopys, approval _____
39. wierd, stately _____
40. forgetable, hurried _____

Spelling 2

Use the spelling words listed on pages 666–667 in *Write Source* to complete this exercise.

> **Underline** each misspelled word below and write the correct spelling above it.

really

1. The world's first roads were <u>realy</u> trails made by game animals and by the

2. hunters who undoutably followed them. After the wheel was invented (about

3. 3000 B.C.E.), roads typically followed trade routs.

4.   The Romans were the first great road builders, althogh other civilezations

5. had built roads previosly. The Romans laid a solid base and braught in flat

6. stones for pavement. They concieved a plan for water drainage. They made sure

7. the roads sloped adequetely from the center to both sides, and they constructed

8. ditches to carry the water away.

9.   Although French enginears used gravel and stone on some roads in the

10. 1700s, most roads remained little more than a clearing of mud until the 1800s.

11. It was then—during the Industral Revolution—that a road surface called

12. *macadam* (small stones packed into layers) was developped. Macadam is still

13. utillized on some roads today.

14.   In the early 1900s, the demand for good roads increased. With the

15. introduction of the automobele, well-built streets were no longer a luxsury; they

16. were a necesity. Few United States highways were constructed, however, until

17. after the Great Depression of the 1930s. In 1956, the imense federel interstate

18. highway system was implemented. Nearly 40 years later, the work was complete

19. exept, of course, for that anual anoyance called "construction season."

Extend: Explain to a classmate the spelling rules (or the exceptions) you used to make four of the corrections in the sentences above.

Spelling 3

Turn to page 688 in *Write Source* to find spelling rules that will help you with this exercise. Also refer to the list of commonly misspelled words on pages 666–667 to find correct spellings of many of the words.

> **Underline** each misspelled word below and write the correct spelling above it.

                   imagine

1   When you <u>imagin</u> a panda, you probly picture a large, likeable, cuddly

2   bear that has a white face with a black patch around each eye. That's a

3   *giant panda,* and it's enormus—with an average heit of five to six feet and

4   an average wieght of 200 to 300 pounds.

5   But there is a diffrent species of panda, called the red panda, whose

6   appearence more closely resembles a raccoon's. A red panda has long, soft,

7   redish fur and a bushy tail with rings. It wieghs only about 11 pounds,

8   and its body measures about two feet in lenth.

9   Both species of panda live in the bamboo forests of China. The red

10   panda has three other habittats as well: the bamboo forests of northern

11   India, Myanmar, and Nepal. Each species must eat substansial quantitys

12   of bamboo. In fact, the giant panda offen consumes 85 pounds each day!

13   So, how are pandas classifyed? Should they be part of the bear family

14   or the raccoon family? Actually, zoologists disagree—not only on how

15   pandas should be classified but also on the issue of how closely the two

16   species are related. Some scientists reconize that the DNA of red pandas

17   is similer to that of raccoons, while the DNA of giant pandas paralels

18   that of bears. Perhaps these creatures—both red and giant pandas—

19   deserve a seperate family of their own.

Spelling 4

Refer to the list of commonly misspelled words on pages 666–667 in *Write Source* for help with this exercise.

> **Underline** each misspelled word in the news story below and write the correct spelling above.

Grocery

1   The latest fire to hit Oakton this month destroyed the Streetside <u>Grosery</u>

2   Store. Forchunately, no one was injured.

3   Oakton Fire Chief Flynn stated, "There will be an inquirey into this fire,

4   as it is of suspitious origin. The beureau will conduct a thurough investigation."

5   "The reckage caused by the fire won't be safe to remove for several days,"

6   Leutenant Wills remarked. He also noted that an aquaintance of his, musicien

7   Lamont Burrows, and several family's lost their apartments above the store in

8   the fire.

9   The chief continued, "Although we've been called to eigth fires this month,

10   this one has a eunique pattern. I believe we're dealing with carelessness."

11   Smoke was still thick in the area, and he paused to couph. The basment of the

12   store appears to be the source of the blaze. I think discarded oily rags caused

13   spontainious combustion. People need to realise that trash left lying around

14   can be dangerous. Anyone with any knowlege about when the fire started is

15   requested to contact me."

16   Oakton residents wishing to donate cash, food, close, or misselaneous items

17   to the former ocupants of the building can contact Marilee Singer at Oakton

18   Bank, 555-3200.

Review: Plurals & Spelling

> **Write** the correct plural for each word that appears in parentheses.

1. The _____*people*_____ (person) went to the _____

(city) to buy _____ (grocery).

2. The _____ (wife) of the _____ (director)

decided that they would try out for the _____ (solo).

3. The _____ (patio) on the _____ (house)

need new _____ (brick).

4. The _____ (belief) of the _____ (woman)

differed, but both said the _____ (leaf) could be used for

medicinal _____ (purpose).

5. The _____ (datum) on the _____ (trout)

should be given to the _____ (fishery).

6. There are three _____ (u) in the _____

(name) of my _____ (brother-in-law).

7. The _____ (family) liked the _____ (ox)

and the _____ (monkey).

8. The _____ (story) of the local _____ (hero)

were very interesting to the _____ (class).

9. The _____ (roof) of the abandoned _____

(factory) are in terrible shape.

10. The _____ (banjo) were stolen by _____

(thief) who tried to sell them on the Internet.

Study each group of words listed below. Then, using your own words, write the spelling rule that the word group exemplifies.

1. relieve, believe, receive, sleigh, eight

(See 664.1) Write i before e except after c, or when sounded like a as in neighbor and weigh.

2. likeness, statement, ninety, nineteen

_____

_____

3. hurried, happiness, beautiful, ladies

_____

_____

_____

4. forgettable, committed, occurrence, beginning

_____

_____

_____

5. toys, plays, moneys

_____

_____

6. neither, sheik, weird

_____

_____

7. What should you remember about using a spell checker and a dictionary?

_____

_____

Pretest: Using the Right Word

> **Circle** the correct word (or words) in each group in parentheses in the following paragraphs.

1   (Weather, (Whether)) or not you're a sports fan, you may have heard of Lance

2   Armstrong. He's the cyclist upon *(who, whom)* the eyes of the world were riveted

3   for almost a month in 2005 as he won the Tour de France for the seventh time.

4   This bicycle race ends on the streets of Paris, that country's *(capital, capitol).*

5   Compared to other athletic events, the Tour de France is grueling. It's a 2,303-

6   mile race that requires incredible endurance and stamina. That Armstrong

7   *(chose, choose)* to participate is amazing. After all, some people thought his

8   racing dream was an *(allusion, illusion).*

9   Nine years before, Lance Armstrong learned that he had cancer, and that

10   it was in an advanced stage. But Armstrong did not *(accept, except)* the idea

11   that the disease would *(bring, take)* death. He did not allow the doctor's grim

12   prognosis to *(affect, effect)* his will to live. Instead, Armstrong *(chose, choose)* to

13   fight his disease aggressively, even though the treatments made him feel sick

14   for an entire year. *(Among, Between)* cancer survivors, Armstrong is a hero.

15   Another athlete who faced cancer and did not give up is Sweden's first gold-

16   medal winner in track and field, Lyudmila Engquist. After her cancer surgery and

17   treatment, she felt *(good, well)* enough to win the 100-meter hurdles in Stockholm.

18   Of course, Armstrong and Engquist were *(different from, different*

19   *than)* most people. They were both athletes in *(peak, pique, peek)* physical

20   condition. Then *(to, too, two),* their *(healthful, healthy)* regimens *(complemented,*

21   *complimented)* their genetic makeup. Nevertheless, *(their, there, they're)* successes

22   challenge everyone to look at cancer differently.

Using the Right Word 1

Fill in the blanks from the list below to correctly complete the sentences. See *Write Source* pages 678, 680, and 682.

accept, except; adapt, adopt; affect, effect; allusion, illusion; among, between; amount, number; ascent, assent; bad, badly; base, bass; bring, take; capital, capitol; choose, chose

1. After studying the hitting and fielding records of each player, Coach Silvan decided to ____*choose*____ Armin.

2. During the building of the Panama Canal, engineers used several methods to control the _____ of mosquitoes.

3. Many mountaineers make the _____ of Mt. Everest their ultimate goal.

4. The director knew that Spuriel's powerful _____ voice was a wonderful addition to the school glee club.

5. Jerome was asked to _____ the broken glass to the trash bin.

6. In the 1800s, the American Plains Indians were thought to be _____ the finest horse riders in the world.

7. Because he fell off the parallel bars during a complicated routine, Central High's star gymnast suffered a _____ broken forearm.

8. When the comet Shoemaker-Levy collided with Jupiter, the _____ startled and amazed astronomers.

9. Realizing funds were limited, the student council decided to _____ a simpler and cheaper plan for the homecoming dance.

10. Everyone _____ Shane saw the lightning bolt splinter the power pole.

11. Jan's _____ to what she might like for her birthday did not go unnoticed by her brother.

12. Denver, often called the "Mile-high City," is the _____ of Colorado.

Using the Right Word 2

Turn to pages 684–687 in *Write Source* for help with this exercise.

> **Write** the correction above each underlined word that is misused. Write **C** above each underlined word that's used correctly.

1   People who decide to immigrate from their homelands seek a new

2   beginning for themselves and new opportunities for their families. Such

3   people believe that in spite of the risks and the challenges their families

4   will face, the change will be well. Immigrants quickly discover that

5   regulations in the "new" country are different from those in the "old."

6   Countries often require that newcomers be healthy. These nations

7   may check farther into the backgrounds of the new arrivals than might

8   normally be expected. Immigrants are unsure about what authorities might

9   imply from the answers to the immigration questions. For United States

10   officials, immigration has been a continuous process.

11   Many citizens feel that people who come to the Unted States are

12   paying this country a grand complement. Of coarse, some feel that

13   immigration should be drastically reduced. As far as they are concerned,

14   the new people take too many jobs. They believe the newcomers make it

15   harder for natural-born citizens to find work.

16   The truth is that most of the time, those who immigrate have been

17   good for the United States. The immigrants' flare for doing a good job and

18   for sharing ideas has helped make this country successful.

Extend: Write your own sentences using the following words correctly: *counsel, desert, fewer,* and *idle*.

Using the Right Word 3

Turn to pages 688–693 in *Write Source*.

> **Underline** each usage error in the passage below and write the correction above it.

1. After watching 15 fellow skiers try and then fail to beat his time, Jeffrey could
scarcely believe that the gold <u>meddle</u> belonged to him.
medal (above meddle)

2. What made the victory special was knowing that every one of these skiers had
trained daily like he had.

3. From a very early age, Jeffrey's interest had been peaked by competition.

4. When he began his quest, he quickly learned that winning gold would come
from his metal more than from his skill.

5. He would lay back at the base of the hill to watch skiers make their runs.

6. Jeffrey would peace together the best route, and then practice running it.

7. The constant practice, the troubling injuries, and the difficult race schedule
sometimes made him want to quite.

8. However, the sight of a snow-covered peek would suddenly send a rush of
adrenaline through him, and he would be ready to go again.

9. Jeffrey once said, "For me, its not the competition against others; its the
challenge to overcome my own uncertainties."

10. Jeffrey learned all he could about his equipment so that he could insure that it
was in it's best condition.

11. His family and friends provided the moral boost he needed when it appeared he
would be eliminated.

12. Jeffrey peaked at the gold medallion and happily waved to the cheering crowd.

Extend: Write a sentence for each of the following words: *plain, like, insure,* and *meddle.*

Using the Right Word 4

Turn to pages 694–697 in *Write Source*.

> **Underline** each usage error in the passage below and write the correction above it.

sight

1   The cite of a hummingbird hovering close to a brightly colored flower

2   attracts the attention of even the most disinterested person. There is something

3   real special about these tiny flying gems, and your just as likely to be

4   fascinated by their tiny size as their ability to fly backward.

5   Most people know that hummingbirds seek nectar, but many people do

6   not know hummingbirds may eat up to 500 bugs per day. When the whether

7   turns rainy, hummingbirds eat even more. They are vary fond of eating what

8   we would call vial-tasting spiders and flying insects. To attract these birds, use

9   a bright red or yellow feeder. The rite food to put in the feeder is concentrated

10 sugar water, who does not have to be red to attract hummingbirds.

11 Hummingbirds very in size from 2 1/4 inches to 8 1/2 inches. In North

12 America, you will look in vane for the largest bird because it only lives in South

13 America. Although hummingbirds seem very frail, they can be found as far

14 north as Alaska and as far south as the tip of South America, both real cold

15 places.

16 The person that wants to observe hummingbirds should put up a feeder

17 and plant many flowers. One quote from a bird book states that hummingbirds

18 are fearless and will feed at a feeder even if a person stands close by. Watch

19 these birds and than take pictures of these winged jewels.

Extend: Write your own sentences using the following words correctly: *stationary, vain, waist,* and *whom.*

Review: Using the Right Word

> **Underline** each usage error in the sentences below and write the correction above it.

          illusions

1. Do you have any <u>allusions</u> about what Alaska will be like?

2. Of coarse! But I'm rite when I say I'm ready for my Alaska experience.

3. If I'm wrong, I'll adopt my behavior as necessary.

4. My cousin will leave me use his heavy parka and snowshoes.

5. I plan to spend next year attending school in Anchorage, which should be a real

enjoyable experience.

6. I expect to do a lot of hiking, so I'm bringing my camera.

7. Alaska has too many trails for me to hike in just one year, but there are

an amount of trails that I have chosen to hike no matter what.

8. Will I like the long Alaskan winter? Actually, I look forward to some real

winter whether.

9. I choose several books to bring; they're ones I've been wanting to read.

10. My cousin, who lives in Anchorage, says she often sees moose wander down a

street and then lay down in someone's backyard.

11. Ever since I was little, my dream to live in Alaska did not very.

12. I hope I see a large number of snow-covered peeks.

13. The pictures that I've seen in books infer incredible beauty, but I know it's even

better to stand before a glacier or at the foot of a mountain.

14. I don't know if I'll get to the capitol city of Juneau like my brother did.

15. The year will pass much too fast, I expect, and than I'll have to let many new

friends and favorite places behind.

Review: Proofreading Activities

> **Choose** the punctuation in column B that can be used in the manner described in column A. Then write the letter in the blank.

Column A

_____ **1.** Joins prefixes like "self" to words

_____ **2.** Separates equal adjectives

_____ **3.** Set off titles of songs, short stories, and magazine articles

_____ **4.** Sets off the names of books, ships, and TV programs

_____ **5.** Used in a series if commas are already used

_____ **6.** Used to set off a word, a phrase, or a clause from the rest of the sentence (for emphasis)

_____ **7.** Used in contractions

_____ **8.** Ends an interrogative sentence

_____ **9.** Ends an exclamatory sentence

_____ **10.** Ends a declarative sentence

Column B

a. Comma

b. Apostrophe

c. Dash or colon

d. Quotation marks

e. Question mark

f. Hyphen

g. Period

h. Semicolon

i. Italics (Underlining)

j. Exclamation point

> **Proofread** the sentences below. Correct the errors in spelling or usage.

1. You're *right* <u>write!</u> These personal questions are embarrasing and not

appropriate.

2. Even fourty spoonsful of sugar wouldn't make this medicine go down.

3. Throughly checking the brakes on your car is the begining of automobile

saftey, and its a real good idea.

4. Lay down and relax. These boys will play the banjoes as good as they can.

5. Whom will be in charge of recieving the moral-boosting guest of honor?

6. The visitor's unforgetable story had a chilling affect on everyone who

choose to listen.

Proofread the essay below. Cross out any error you find in capitalization, numbers, plurals, and usage. Write the correction above it. Add or fix punctuation as necessary.

1   My friends Millie and Sarah say The small earth-friendly recycling

2   you do each each day really adds up. For example you can recycle the

3   cardboard cylinders that are found in these items gift wrap paper toweling

4   plastic wrap waxed paper and aluminum foil.

5   Sarah, who's a whiz at crafts, says, Or maybe youd rather reuse these

6   tubes. Everyone can use an extra necktie or scarf rack, or a

7   custom-made window shade the cardboard tube becomes a dowel for it.

8   And why not make a cardboard napkin ring or sachet you could even

9   make a cookie cutter.

10 Cardboard tubes are not the only useful item's to recycle Millie

11 claims that containers such as jars, bottles, empty nut canisters, waxed

12 cardboard, milk containers, and aluminum coffee cans can all be reused

13 Old coffee cans can be used as safety lights just place strip's of bright

14 reflector tape on the cans then put them in the trunk of your car for an

15 emergency.

16 with these items and your creative ability, you can make simple lamp

17 basses, hassocks, planters, tool chests, and even canisters to hold writing

18 supplies! Millie exclaims. Speaking of VCRs, Millie and Sarah also have

19 an idea on how to reuse videotape. If youve found a wornout videotape

20 in your collection pull the tape out of it's casing. Glue small handmade

21 snowflakes on the tape at 5 inch intervals. Voila you have garland for

22 your doorway.

Parts of Speech Activities

The activities in this section provide a review of the different parts of speech. Most of the activities also include helpful textbook references. In addition, the Extend activities encourage follow-up practice of certain skills.

Types of Nouns 2

The number of a noun indicates whether it's singular (one *potato,* one *person*) or plural (two *potatoes,* several *people*). A concrete noun names a thing that is tangible, while an abstract noun names an idea, a condition, or a feeling. Turn to 702.1, 701.3, and 701.4 in *Write Source.*

> **Underline** the words used as nouns below. Write **S** above each singular noun and **P** above each plural noun.

            S

1. My <u>school</u> recently underwent some unusual construction.

2. Supervisors and workmen swarmed through the building.

3. Scaffolds surrounded the six floors of the building.

4. The old doors and windows that had been damaged in a storm had to be removed and replaced.

5. Workers hammered and ran power tools on scaffolds outside classroom windows.

6. Students and teachers found it hard not to watch the workers.

> **Underline** the nouns below. Write **A** above each abstract noun and **C** above each concrete noun.

1. The winter weather complicated and prolonged the construction work.

2. Workers carefully negotiated the slippery scaffolds and struggled to maintain their balance in the freezing gusts of wind.

3. School staff and construction workers alike celebrated the installation of the final window.

4. Our principal invited the workers to the cafeteria for sandwiches and coffee.

5. The construction team was just as happy as we were that the midyear project was over.

Extend: Write two sentences for each of these collective nouns: *crowd, faculty,* and *group.* In the first sentence, make the noun singular (it refers to the group as a unit). In the second sentence, make the noun plural (it refers to the individuals within the group).

Functions of Nouns

There are six different uses for nouns (see the chart below). Turn to the appropriate references in *Write Source* for information.

Write Source	Function	Symbol	Example
738.1	subject	**S**	*Children* play.
702.3	predicate noun	**PN**	Bobby is only a *child*.
716.2	possessive noun	**POS**	A *child's* voice cried out.
716.2	direct object	**DO**	Someone had accidentally kicked the *child*.
732	indirect object	**IO**	We gave the *child* an adhesive bandage.
702.3	object of preposition	**OP**	The other children gathered near the *child*.

Using the symbols from the chart above, label the function of the underlined nouns in the following sentences.

1. Cremation is the final arrangement for the dead in Buddhist and Hindu regions of the world and is becoming more common in the United States and Canada.

2. Some cultures have other methods for taking care of their dead; in Tibet, a water burial is customary.

3. The ancient Egyptians placed their dead in tombs with food, jewels, and other things.

4. They mummified the dead, as they believed the body's spirit would return to it.

5. The tradition of burying the dead developed from a common belief in "coming back"—that the body is a seed to be planted in the earth to await rebirth.

6. Cemeteries provide people a special place to bury and memorialize the dead.

7. Arlington National Cemetery covers more than 600 acres in Arlington, Virginia.

8. It is probably the most famous cemetery in the United States.

9. The only presidents buried there are John Kennedy and William Taft.

10. Marked by an eternal flame, the grave of JFK is visited by thousands of people each year.

Nominative, Possessive, & Objective Cases of Nouns

In the *nominative case,* a noun is used as the subject or the predicate nominative. In the *possessive case,* the noun shows ownership or possession. In the *objective case,* the noun is used as the direct object, the indirect object, or the object of a preposition. Turn to 702.3 in *Write Source.*

Indicate whether each underlined noun is in the nominative case (*N*), the possessive case (*P*), or the objective case (*O*).

___*O*___ **1.** Scientists have dreamed of many different <u>designs</u> for tomorrow's spacecraft.

_____ **2.** Some designs resemble the spacecraft used today that burn chemical fuel for <u>propulsion</u>.

_____ **3.** Other futuristic <u>craft</u> are powered by controlled nuclear explosions. (Those spaceships could take people to Mars in half the time!)

_____ **4.** One scientist's design beams power out to spacecraft using a high-powered <u>laser</u> that orbits Earth.

_____ **5.** A few <u>concepts</u> have spacecraft sailing on the "solar wind" of tiny particles expelled by the sun.

_____ **6.** But astronauts' <u>journeys</u> to other solar systems will still be incredibly long, so early interstellar travelers may have to travel frozen in suspended animation.

Write sentences using each of the following nouns in the indicated cases.

1. Mars *(nominative):* _____

_____

2. Earth *(possessive):* _____

_____

3. aliens *(objective):* _____

_____

4. space station *(objective):* _____

_____

Extend: Rewrite each of your sentences using each of the listed nouns in a different case.

Specific Nouns

Strong, specific nouns are essential for clear communication and lively writing. For example, you would probably be excited if you found out that you had won a car in a drawing! However, your excitement would increase if they told you that you had won a sports car—in fact, let's say it's a convertible! A specific noun makes a big difference. Turn to pages 74 and 701.3–701.4 in *Write Source*.

Write a sentence containing a noun that fits each description below. Circle this noun. Be as specific and vivid as possible!

1. plural, proper, thing: _A recent ad campaign has boosted the_ _popularity of (Chihuahuas) as family pets._

2. singular, concrete, thing: _____

3. collective, proper, people: _____

4. singular, abstract, idea: _____

5. singular, proper, place: _____

6. plural, concrete, thing: _____

7. singular, proper, person: _____

8. plural, common, thing: _____

9. singular, abstract, idea: _____

Review: Nouns

_S_ _A_   **1.** Snowboarding has exploded onto the international sports scene, attracting weekend skiers and extreme athletes alike.

___ ___   **2.** The sport was originally known as "snurfing," a combination of the words "snow" and "surfing."

___ ___   **3.** Sherman Poppen invented the "snurfer" in 1965; after his daughter tried to sled standing up, he screwed two skis together.

___ ___   **4.** Many entrepreneurs tried to design a better way to surf on now, but it wasn't until 1977—when Jake Burton Carpenter attached rubber bootstraps to a wooden board and coated it with plastic— that the modern snowboard was born.

___ ___   **5.** Jake Burton Carpenter's design led to the creation of one of the most famous snowboarding companies in existence: Burton.

___ ___   **6.** The popularity of snowboarding increased dramatically in the 1980s when snowboarding companies held international competitions.

___ ___   **7.** American snowboarders also formed the U.S. Amateur Snowboard Association (USASA) in the '80s.

___ ___   **8.** When ESPN televised the Winter X Games in the '90s, they were the first major network to televise extreme sports competitions.

___ ___   **9.** Twenty years after Burton had created his first board, in 1998, snowboarding became an official Olympic sport.

___ ___ **10.** Snowboarders from around the world gave the spectators and viewers outstanding performances competing for medals at the Winter Olympics in Salt Lake City, Utah.

Pretest: Pronouns

Circle the correct pronoun in each pair below.

1. Many of *(us, we)* Americans have relatives or ancestors who have come to this country from other places on the globe.

2. How many American citizens do you know *(who, whom)* were born outside the United States?

3. Have you ever wondered why so many people leave *(his or her, their)* native lands to come here?

4. Between you and *(I, me)*, I can't imagine permanently leaving the country where I grew up.

5. Emigrants, *(who, which)* leave their native land, often agonize over the decision.

6. In one way or another, people *(who, which)* come to America are seeking a better life for *(himself, themselves)* and for *(their, his or her)* children.

7. People for *(who, whom)* citizenship is a goal must be at least 18 years old, and they must be able to understand English if *(they are, he or she is)* under age 55.

8. My neighbor, Juan Planas, who is trying to improve his English, always has a question for my brother and *(I, me)*.

9. "It is *(I, me)*, Juan," he always says proudly—and correctly—as he answers the phone.

10. Juan says that *(his, their)* naturalization test included questions on American government that many native-born Americans would not be able to answer.

11. He bought *(hisself, himself)* a United States almanac to read, supplementing the basic study materials that every prospective citizen receives.

Personal Pronouns

Pronouns are words used in place of nouns. All pronouns have antecedents (the noun that the pronoun refers to or replaces). Turn to page 704 in *Write Source* for further details.

> **Underline** the personal pronoun in each sentence. If the pronoun's antecedent is in the same sentence, circle it.

1. (Anne Rice) is known for <u>her</u> popular novels about vampires.

2. The author has been praised for making her supernatural characters seem believable.

3. Stephen King is another author of mystical novels, and his books are often best-sellers.

4. King's stories deal with horrifying events that he makes happen amid an everyday setting—something bound to scare us.

5. Several of King's stories take place in Maine, a state where he continues to live.

6. King was a schoolteacher before he turned to writing full-time.

7. King is one of my favorite authors.

8. Perhaps you are familiar with Edgar Allan Poe or R. L. Stine.

9. Poe and Stine are also authors of supernatural tales; their horror stories are some of the oldest and newest of the genre.

10. Manny and I read many of Stine's books—we love to be frightened!

11. Another way Manny and I scare ourselves is to go on carnival rides.

12. I do not trust the safety of some of the rides.

13. A friend broke his finger while exiting a roller coaster.

14. Once Manny did not feel well after he rode one of the rides.

15. But the designers of such rides continue to make them as scary as possible!

Extend: Write five sentences about your favorite novel, class, or amusement park ride. Include at least one personal pronoun in each sentence.

Number & Person of Personal Pronouns

Personal pronouns are either singular or plural in number. A pronoun can be one of three persons: *first* (the person is speaking), *second* (is spoken to), or *third* (is spoken about). Turn to 708.1–708.2 in *Write Source*.

> **Underline** and label the personal pronouns in the following sentences. Label each pronoun twice: use an **S** (singular) or a **P** (plural); also use a **1** (first person), **2** (second person), or **3** (third person).

1. "Lauren, <u>your</u> dog needs a bath!" Mom said to <u>my</u> little sister.
              S/2   *S/1*

2. We chased it and put it in the tub.

3. The minutes passed slowly as he watched the clock.

4. With a sly smile, the teacher informed us, "You are free to go."

5. Upon hearing his statement, we streamed out of the classroom.

6. "Dynice, is this your backpack?" José asked.

> **Insert** a personal pronoun in the blanks below so that each sentence makes sense. Label your pronouns in the same way you did in the exercise above. (Label *you* **S/P** because it can be singular or plural.)

1. _____We_____ are going on a vacation this summer. *P/1*

2. Will _____ be visiting any relatives?

3. After the movie, _____ am going to get something to eat.

4. _____ is taking a typing class.

5. _____ asked _____ if _____ wanted to join _____ .

6. Dad said _____ would help _____ make dinner.

7. _____ decided to make spaghetti, but _____ forgot to watch the pot and _____ boiled over.

Extend: Write three to five sentences about your friends. Try to use first-, second-, and third-person pronouns in both singular and plural forms.

Functions of Pronouns

Pronouns function the same way that nouns do (see the chart below). Turn to 710.1—and to the other sections listed in the first column below—for further information.

Write Source	Function	Symbol	Example
738.1	*subject*	**S**	Will *you* please feed the cat?
710.1	*predicate nominative*	**PN**	The winner is *he*.
740.1	*possessive pronoun*	**POS**	He lost *his* book bag.
710.1	*direct object*	**DO**	Magda is driving *me* to school.
710.1	*indirect object*	**IO**	Julian told *her* a secret.
732	*object of preposition*	**OP**	The bus stopped right in front of *us*.

> **Identify** the function of the underlined pronouns in the sentences below, using the symbols from the chart above.

                      POS

1. I believe you've got <u>my</u> book, and I want <u>it</u> back.

2. Does this bracelet belong to <u>you</u> or to <u>her</u>?

3. Come with <u>me</u>.

4. "The winner was <u>she</u>," Ronald pointed out when <u>he</u> saw the runners.

5. "<u>It</u> is not <u>mine</u>," said Mr. Grenoble.

6. Grandpa gave <u>them</u> a piece of <u>his</u> mind.

7. <u>She</u> was surprised to learn that <u>he</u> wore a toupee.

8. In addition to <u>me</u>, <u>my</u> sister and <u>her</u> friend participated in the neighborhood cleanup.

9. I gave <u>him</u> a haircut, but <u>he</u> didn't like <u>it</u>.

10. The unmarked police vehicle had <u>its</u> lights flashing.

11. Tara thought Russell was choosing <u>her</u> for <u>his</u> team.

12. The victory was <u>theirs</u> until <u>he</u> fumbled the ball.

Extend: Write four to six sentences about your typical day. Include pronouns in each sentence; try to use at least three of the six functions listed in the chart above.

Nominative, Possessive, & Objective Cases of Pronouns

The case of each personal pronoun tells how it is related to the other words used with it. There are three cases: *nominative, possessive,* and *objective.* Turn to 710.1 in *Write Source.*

> **Underline** the personal pronouns below. Then identify each pronoun on the line, using **N** for nominative, **POS** for possessive, or **O** for objective.

_N_ **1.** I went to Malaysia last summer.

_____ **2.** My luggage was lost on the way.

_____ **3.** How could this happen to me?

_____ **4.** We landed in the capital, Kuala Lumpur, Malaysia's largest city.

_____ **5.** Cindy went with her tour group to Mount Kinabalu, the highest mountain in Malaysia.

_____ **6.** I went with another group to see an archeological site.

_____ **7.** We learned that Malaysia's government is modeled after the British government.

_____ **8.** Our group also learned that most Malaysians speak English well.

_____ **9.** Mike toured a rubber plantation and later wrote a paper about his experience.

_____ **10.** The tour guide told us a great deal about Malaysia's economy.

_____ **11.** "Malaysia is one of the world's largest producers of tin," she said.

_____ **12.** The people who went with her had fun.

_____ **13.** This trip taught me a lot about Malaysia.

_____ **14.** Our itinerary included many historic sites.

_____ **15.** The Malaysian people are proud of their country.

_____ **16.** Tourists often marvel at its exotic beauty.

Extend: Write five to eight sentences about a place you have visited. Before you get started, figure out which personal pronouns were not used in the exercise above (they, them, etc.). Put them in your sentences. (See the personal pronouns on the chart on 710.1.)

Reflexive & Intensive Pronouns

Both reflexive and intensive pronouns are formed by adding *-self* or *-selves* to a personal pronoun. Turn to 706.1 in *Write Source* for more information.

> Reflexive Pronoun: Cassie hurt *herself* by lifting a 50-pound dumbbell.

> Intensive Pronoun: The mayor *herself* gave us a tour of city hall.

> **Underline** each reflexive pronoun and write *R* above it. Underline each intensive pronoun and label it *I*.

1. Fabio found <u>himself</u> [R] longing for a Mohawk haircut.

2. Not even Batman himself could have saved us.

3. The material was difficult, but the test itself was easy.

4. The gerbil gave itself quite a shock from the static electricity.

5. Yes, I have learned that myself.

6. The students looked at themselves as they walked by the crazy mirror.

7. We ourselves cannot imagine a brighter future for polyester.

8. You should see yourselves! You're burnt to a crisp.

9. Can you yourself honestly say it never happened?

10. Paula has not been herself since the incident.

> **Write** five short sentences, each using a different reflexive or intensive pronoun.

1. _____
2. _____
3. _____
4. _____
5. _____

Extend: Return to the sentences you just wrote. Write an *R* above each reflexive pronoun and an *I* above each intensive pronoun.

Relative Pronouns

A relative pronoun relates an adjective clause to the noun or pronoun it modifies. Turn to 728.2 and see the chart on page 704 in *Write Source*.

 I loved to watch the dolphins *that were following our boat*. (*Dolphins* is the noun, and *that* is the relative pronoun. The adjective clause is in italics.)

> **Circle** each relative pronoun. Then underline the noun or pronoun that each relative pronoun relates to.

1. Writing (that) is good requires time and attention.

2. People who fish usually do not enjoy seeing water snakes.

3. I marvel at bird behaviors—their songs, their flight patterns, their nest building, their migration—which often seem beyond explanation.

4. Mr. and Mrs. Smith, whose egos prevent them from enjoying the simple successes of others, were our neighbors.

5. The wolfhound that won the prize was raised in Ireland.

6. The thieves who robbed the train were caught when the train stopped.

7. The cleanup committee picked up all the garbage, which was later taken to the recycling center.

8. Put that book, which is a priceless copy of a first edition, on the top shelf.

9. These are the socks that have holes in the toes.

10. Blair was seated next to that man, whom he thinks is clever.

11. This is a breed of dog that loves people unconditionally.

12. Where is the birthday present that you received from your friend?

13. Were you the one who tied the yellow ribbon to the tree?

14. Make me a promise that you can keep.

Extend: Notice where commas are used above. In a brief paragraph, explain the rule for using commas with restrictive and nonrestrictive clauses. (To review the definition of restrictive and nonrestrictive clauses, see 612.2 in *Write Source*.)

Relative Pronouns in Subordinate Clauses

Who, whom, which, whose, and *that* are relative pronouns. Writers use them to modify or subordinate (to give one idea in a sentence less importance) a noun or pronoun. Turn to 706.2 in *Write Source.*

> **Combine** the pairs of sentences below into one sentence. Use a relative pronoun to modify a noun in the main clause or to subordinate the less important idea.

1. An experiment does not deserve federal funding. The experiment does nothing to serve the public interest.

An experiment that does nothing to serve the public interest does not

deserve federal funding.

2. At midnight, the Duvalls were ticketed for making noise over 120 decibels. The Duvalls were celebrating Mardi Gras.

_____

_____

3. I knew the comb didn't belong to the policeman. The policeman's hat had blown off, revealing a completely bald head.

_____

_____

_____

4. A small group of guests made absolute fools of themselves. The guests had been practicing their comedy routines.

_____

_____

_____

5. The accident left her paralyzed. The accident happened a year ago today.

_____

_____

Indefinite, Interrogative, & Demonstrative Pronouns

Indefinite pronouns refer to unnamed or unknown people or things and usually have an unknown antecedent. Interrogative pronouns ask questions, and demonstrative pronouns point out people, places, or things without naming them. Turn to 706.4 in *Write Source*. Also turn to page 696 for information about "*who*" and "*whom*."

Write the missing interrogative pronoun in each blank below.

1. She shopped on Second Avenue. _____ store did she visit?

2. Aaron's bike is in the garage. _____ bike is behind the house?

3. Elena invited Ted, but _____ invited Elena?

Add the missing demonstrative pronouns.

1. The hat is huge. Can you actually wear _____ on a hike?

2. Those apples look wormy. I'll eat _____ instead.

3. Holding up an astrolabe, she asked, "Do you know what _____ is?"

Underline each indefinite pronoun.

1. Everyone knows that Ben Franklin was a powerful statesman.

2. Few know that he also was an inventor, a printer, a public servant, and a writer.

3. Do you know anyone who wrote his or her own epitaph?

4. The Continental Congress named several of its members to draft the Declaration of Independence.

5. Franklin, Jefferson, and Adams proposed the motto on the Great Seal, "One out of many."

6. Somebody wanted Congress to declare Franklin's birthday a national holiday.

7. Nothing would make me happier! (Okay, so maybe something would. . . .)

Review: Pronouns

                                                                         R

1   Sometime in the seventh century—nearly 1,400 years ago—monks, <u>who</u>

2   were translating books from Latin, wrote notes in the margins. They wanted to

3   be certain everyone would know the meaning of their translations. The margin

4   notes came to be called *glosses,* from which we get the word *glossary.*

5   Around 1600, an Englishman named Robert Cawdrey published *A Table*

6   *Alphabeticall of Hard English Wordes.* What is he remembered for? As one might

7   guess, he listed the words in alphabetical order. That might not sound like a big

8   deal now, but it was in 1600 when nobody else had done so.

9   In 1721, Nathan Bailey created his own version of the dictionary. This

10   included a history of words—a distinction that helped make Bailey's book a

11   best-seller. Publishers reprinted it 30 times.

1.   *they*   P, 3, N   5. _____

2. _____   6. _____

3. _____   7. _____

4. _____   8. _____

Pretest: Verbs

> **Underline** all the main, helping, and linking verbs in the following passage.

1   The United States Customs Department <u>needs</u> good dogs. The Customs
2 Department trains dogs to sniff out illegal narcotics at airports and other
3 ports of entry. Ninety percent of the department's dogs have come from animal
4 shelters. A trained narcotics dog is a good hunter. Aggressive dogs can frighten
5 travelers and are not chosen by customs officials for narcotics work. The
6 department's beagles at O'Hare International Airport in Chicago have become
7 an attraction. The dogs are known as the "Beagle Brigade." Travelers chuckle
8 when seeing the cute canines. One German woman did not want to leave the
9 customs area—even though she had spent nine hours on a flight—because she
10 wanted to see the "Beagle Brigade." I understood. I saw them once, and now
11 I always hope they will be on duty when I meet friends at the international
12 terminal.

> **Provide** the following information from the paragraph above. Always list the words for your answers in the order in which they appear in the paragraph.

1. List five of the nine present tense verbs. *needs, trains, is, can frighten, are*
chosen, are known, chuckle, hope, meet

2. List two of the four past tense verbs. _____

3. List the one future tense verb. _____

4. List five of the eight helping (auxiliary) verbs. _____

_____

5. The two helping verbs _____ and _____ are used to form

perfect verb tenses.

6. The one linking verb in line 4 connects the subject _____ with the

predicate nominative _____ .

7. What is the direct object in line 1? _____

8. What verbal is used in line 2? _____

Main Verbs & Auxiliary Verbs

Verbs are words that express action (*crumble, run, think*). Auxiliary verbs, or helping verbs, help form tenses (*had* crumbled, *will* run, *did* think) as well as the passive voice (*was* crumbled) and some moods (*were* to crumble). Turn to page 714 in *Write Source* for information and a list of common auxiliary verbs.

> **Underline** all the verbs below. When an auxiliary verb is used, underline it twice.

1. Germany ranks second in population among the European countries.

2. It is growing at a rate of less than 1 percent annually.

3. In 1949, Germany was split into two different countries.

4. A communist government controlled East Germany from 1949 until the Berlin Wall was toppled in 1989.

5. On October 3, 1990, East and West Germany were officially reunited into one nation.

6. Most people agree that Germany has become one of Europe's most powerful economic leaders.

7. Germans enjoy one of the highest standards of living in Europe.

8. Germany's economy is going through many changes.

9. Germans have a rich cultural heritage that includes many famous writers, artists, composers, conductors, and philosophers.

10. Many forms of German culture and fine art are subsidized by public funds.

11. German students pursue one of three different tracks of schooling, depending upon their interests and academic skills.

12. Science education ranks at the forefront in German schools.

13. German scientists won more Nobel Prizes than scientists from any other country between 1900 and 1933.

14. Germans have decided that science will contribute most to their economic future.

Linking Verbs, Predicate Nouns, & Predicate Adjectives

A linking verb "links" a subject to a predicate noun (she *is* a carpenter) or a predicate adjective (she *looks* strong). Rather than describing an action, linking verbs describe a condition or a state of being. Turn to 714.1 in *Write Source* for examples.

> **Underline** the linking verb in each sentence below. Label each predicate noun **PN** and each predicate adjective **PA**.

1. The lemonade <u>tasted</u> so good. *PA*

2. I am allergic to peanuts.

3. My old house is drafty and homely.

4. My old house remains my castle.

5. The mustangs in the parking lot are horses, not autos.

6. Miss Catchpaw feels ill.

7. My sisters were the contest judges.

8. I'm very sleepy.

9. You look marvelous!

10. Cigarette smoke smells awful.

> **Compose** sentences with linking verbs, following the directions below.

1. Use the linking verb *are* to connect a subject with a predicate noun.

_____

2. Use the linking verb *seems* to connect a subject with a predicate adjective.

_____

3. Use a linking verb and a predicate adjective to say something about yourself.

_____

Extend: Make a list of specific nouns and a list of colorful adjectives. Exchange papers with a classmate. Create sentences that use linking verbs to join the nouns to the adjectives.

Strong Nouns & Verbs

By using specific words, you can create clear and colorful word pictures for your readers. Specific nouns and vivid verbs give readers a clearer, more detailed idea of what you are saying. Turn to page 75 in *Write Source* for information.

 George sat down on the seat.

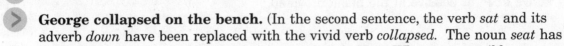 **George collapsed on the bench.** (In the second sentence, the verb *sat* and its adverb *down* have been replaced with the vivid verb *collapsed*. The noun *seat* has been replaced with the more specific noun *bench*. *Note:* Whenever possible, use a verb that is strong enough to stand alone without the help of an adverb.)

> **Write** verbs in the "vivid verb" column below that are stronger than the verbs listed. List "specific nouns" that are stronger than the nouns listed.

Vivid Verbs		**Specific Nouns**	
1. dove	*plunged*	**1.** rain	
2. walked		**2.** room	
3. said		**3.** person	
4. drink		**4.** game	
5. look		**5.** setting	
6. show		**6.** concept	
7. sing		**7.** road	
8. move		**8.** darkness	
9. take		**9.** jewel	
10. throw		**10.** poem	
11. wait		**11.** dance	
12. laugh		**12.** relative	
13. cry		**13.** pasta	

Extend: Write five or six sentences that describe something or someone you know well. Paint a vivid picture in a reader's mind, using vivid action verbs and specific nouns. Exchange papers with a classmate. After reading one another's paper, circle the verbs and nouns that most helped you (the reader) visualize what your partner described.

Active & Passive Voice

Writing in the active voice places your audience closer to the action. Turn to 722.2 in *Write Source* to see just how effective the active voice can be.

> **Identify** the voice of each sentence by underlining the verbs and writing either **A** for active or **P** for passive in the blank provided.

___A___ 1. Wayne Gretzky joined his first hockey team at the age of six.

_____ 2. Record after record was shattered by this young boy.

_____ 3. All over Canada the news was spread.

_____ 4. Fifty goals had been scored by Wayne in a nine-game tournament!

_____ 5. By the time he turned 17 years old, Wayne Gretzky had realized his goal of playing professional hockey.

_____ 6. He always wore the number 9 in honor of his hero Gordie Howe, but he changed to number 99 as a professional player.

_____ 7. The Hart Trophy for the most valuable player was given to Wayne after his rookie season with the Edmonton Oilers.

_____ 8. That same year he was also awarded the Lady Byng Trophy for sportsmanlike conduct.

_____ 9. After winning their fourth championship, the Oilers shocked the hockey world by trading Gretzky to the Los Angeles Kings.

_____ 10. Wayne Gretzky finished his career with the New York Rangers, retiring in 1999 at age 38.

_____ 11. During his years in the National Hockey League, Gretzky held or shared 50 NHL records.

_____ 12. Hockey fans have been amazed by his outstanding play for 21 years.

Extend: Locate all the sentences above that have been written in the passive voice and rewrite them in the active voice.

Present, Past, & Future Tense Verbs

Tense indicates time. The three simple tenses of a verb are present (*I think*), past (*I thought*), and future (*I will think*). Turn to 718.4 in *Write Source*.

Rewrite each sentence below, changing the verb to the tense indicated. (You may change other words as necessary to create a smooth-reading sentence.)

1. Chickadees make nests in our woodland trees.

   Past: _Chickadees made nests in our woodland trees._

   Future: _Chickadees will make nests in our woodland trees._

2. The chickadees were noisy much of the day.

   Present: _____

   Future: _____

3. The chickadees will feed mainly on insects.

   Present: _____

   Past: _____

4. Last year a chickadee nested in an old bluebird house.

   Present: _____

   Future: _____

5. Chickadees will line their nests with fur, feathers, moss, or other soft materials.

   Past: _____

   _____

   Present: _____

   _____

6. The female lays five to eight white eggs with brown spots.

   Past: _____

   Future: _____

Perfect Tense Verbs

Like simple tenses, perfect tenses deal with time. Present perfect, past perfect, and future perfect tenses use helping verbs such as *has, have, had,* and *will have* to form tenses. The past participle of verbs is also needed to form these tenses. To learn about perfect tenses, turn to 720.1 in *Write Source*. Also on 720.2, you will find past participles for irregular verbs.

Write the past participle for each of the present tense verbs listed below. Then write the verb in the perfect tense indicated in parentheses.

Present Tense	Past Participle	Perfect Tense of the Verb
1. begin	*begun*	*(present perfect):* has/have begun
2. drown	_____	*(future perfect):*
3. eat	_____	*(past perfect):*
4. write	_____	*(future perfect):*
5. sing	_____	*(past perfect):*
6. rise	_____	*(present perfect):*
7. bring	_____	*(past perfect):*
8. speak	_____	*(future perfect):*
9. sit	_____	*(present perfect):*
10. hide	_____	*(past perfect):*

Select six of the perfect tenses you created above and use each in a sentence. Be certain you use all three perfect tenses.

1. _____

2. _____

3. _____

4. _____

5. _____

6. _____

All Six Verb Tenses

A writer can express an exact time by selecting one of six verb tenses. To learn more about the "times" that tenses can express, turn to 720.1 and 722.1 in *Write Source*.

> **Write** sentences on the lines below that express the time requested.

1. Use the present tense of *learn* to express action that is happening at the present time.

Broderick learns quickly; I learn slowly.

2. Use the past tense of *learn* to show action completed last week or last month.

_____

3. Use the future tense of *learn* to show action that will take place tomorrow or another future time.

_____

_____

4. Use the present perfect tense of *learn* to show an action that began in the past and is continuing in the present.

_____

_____

5. Use the past perfect tense to show an action in the past that occurs before another past action. (Choose your own verb.)

_____

_____

6. Use the future perfect tense to show action that will begin in the future and be completed by a specific time in the future. (Choose your own verb.)

_____

_____

7. Choose two tenses—either the present, past, or future and a perfect tense—to use in a sentence. (Choose your own verb.)

_____

_____

Extend: Select a short passage from a newspaper or magazine. Underline all the verbs and label the tenses used. Was one tense used more than the others?

Review: Verbs 1

Underline each verb in the sentences below. State the tense and whether the verb is a main verb, a main verb with an auxiliary verb, or a linking verb.

		Tense	Class of Verb
1.	I <u>experienced</u> joy.	*past*	*main verb*
2.	Jane has called.		
3.	They rescued it.		
4.	The sun had set.		
5.	It will work.		
6.	She begins.		
7.	They play.		
8.	She was sick.		
9.	We have eaten.		
10.	It had begun.		
11.	Snow will have fallen.		

Rewrite the following sentences, changing the passive voice to the active voice. Add subjects as needed. Do not change the verb tense.

1. Mistakes were made. *Government officials made mistakes.*

2. Fun was had by many. _____

3. They had been entertained by Phil. _____

_____

4. The decision has been made. _____

5. This show will be aired by the network in the fall. _____

_____

Transitive & Intransitive Verbs

Transitive verbs are followed by a direct object—someone or something that receives the action of the verb. (He *found* gold. He *gave* it away.)

Intransitive verbs are not followed by a direct object. (He *laughed* loudly.) Linking verbs (such as *be, seem, appear*) are always intransitive.

Depending on their meaning, many verbs can be either transitive (I *drove* his new *car*) or intransitive (He *drove* all night). Turn to 716.1 and 716.2 in *Write Source*.

> **Label** each underlined verb in the sentences below with *T* for transitive or *I* for intransitive.

1. The earliest special effects used in movies <u>were</u> incredibly simple.   *I*

2. Editors created lightning by scratching lines directly onto the film.

3. Special-effects crews simulated thunder by rattling sheets of tin, a trick invented for stage plays.

4. In the 1925 movie *The Lost World,* the filmmakers created dinosaurs using "stop-motion animation," shooting one frame at a time and slightly moving the dinosaur models in each frame.

5. Special-effects makeup turned actor Lon Chaney into a mummy, a werewolf, and Frankenstein's monster.

6. As the years passed, Hollywood's bag of tricks to create special effects steadily grew.

7. Snow in June, ghosts in bedrooms, trains barreling off broken bridges—these kinds of special effects have become increasingly realistic, and increasingly complex.

8. With the addition of powerful computers, today's special-effects technicians can do just about anything.

9. One thing still holds true: Only a few years need to pass before "modern" special effects look unrealistic to increasingly sophisticated audiences.

Direct & Indirect Objects

Direct objects and indirect objects receive the action of verbs and are usually nouns or pronouns. A sentence must have a direct object before it can have an indirect object. Turn to 716.2 in *Write Source*.

> **Circle** the verbs in the sentences below. Then, underline and label the direct objects **(DO)** and the indirect objects **(IO)**.

1. The cells of every living organism (contain) <u>genes</u>. *DO*

2. The makeup of each gene determines the organism's traits.

3. Scientists can give an organism different traits with genetic engineering.

4. As a result, genetic engineers can offer medicine, agriculture, and industry new products and procedures.

5. For example, doctors can now give patients insulin that has been manufactured in bacterial "factories."

6. Clinical trials have given doctors good results when gene therapy is used in the treatment of certain disorders.

7. Researchers have offered the pharmaceutical industry genetically engineered microorganisms that break down toxic substances.

8. In the field of agriculture, technicians have genetically engineered small plants to produce a kind of biodegradable plastic.

9. Scottish scientists handed the world an ethics debate in 1996 when they cloned a sheep.

10. Despite its benefits, genetic engineering has caused many people concern.

11. The accidental production of some uncontrollable bacteria may do people harm.

12. Scientists can now manipulate the genetic material of living creatures.

13. Genetics will give us many opportunities for discussion in years to come.

Verbals: Gerunds, Infinitives, & Participles

A verbal is a word that is derived from a verb, but functions as a noun, an adjective, or an adverb. Turn to 726.1–726.3 in *Write Source*.

Type of Verbal	Used as		
	Noun	Adjective	Adverb
Gerund (ends in *-ing*)	X		
Infinitive (introduced by *to*)	X	X	X
Participle (often ends in *-ing* or *-ed*)		X	

Underline the gerunds in the following sentences.

1. Biking through the countryside is a wonderful way to spend a spring afternoon.

2. The summer chore that Aaron likes least is cutting the grass.

3. Sounding like a foghorn, Smitty cleared his throat prior to answering the phone.

Underline the infinitives in the following sentences.

1. A great dream of mine is to write a novel before I turn 30.

2. On his way to the library, he stopped to get a taco and an iced tea.

3. A good reason to drive is to see the sights along the way.

Underline the participles in the following sentences.

1. In this era of suburban sprawl, deer roaming the woods sometimes find themselves grazing in the middle of a homeowner's backyard.

2. The dog's clipped hair was scattered all over the patio.

3. Cars weaving in and out of traffic are menacing on the highway!

4. The condensed version of the speech proved very readable.

Extend: Write three sentences about a topic of your choice. Use each of the three kinds of verbals at least once.

Irregular Verbs 1

The past tense and past participle of a regular verb are usually formed by adding a -d or an -ed. Irregular verbs do not follow this pattern. (I *run*. I *ran*. I have *run*.) Turn to 720.2 in *Write Source*.

> **Complete** the sentences using the past tense or the past participle of the verb given in parentheses.

1. Yesterday I *(am)* _____was_____ an only child; today I have a brother.

2. Jenna and Stephan *(begin)* _____ their packing last night.

3. The committee of citizens *(choose)* _____ a new slogan for our town.

4. He had *(break)* _____ his ankle and needed a ride home.

5. Those bridge builders *(am)* _____ also divers.

6. They have *(dive)* _____ many times to examine a bridge.

7. A clear, deep river *(flow)* _____ past our vacation cabin.

8. Tuckwell Forest in the spring is the most beautiful sight I've ever *(see)* _____ .

9. When we awoke, the waters had *(rise)* _____ three feet!

10. How many people have *(flee)* _____ their homes this past year?

11. We had *(swim)* _____ for more than an hour by 8:00 a.m.

12. The little kid I baby-sit has *(sing)* _____ in a commercial.

13. Mother *(lay)* _____ her purse somewhere and can't find it.

14. The bells have *(ring)* _____ in the church belfry every Easter morning for as long as I can remember.

15. The team has *(wear)* _____ these uniforms for six seasons.

16. Wow, did you see how that little kid *(catch)* _____ that ball?

17. After the international flight, they *(lie)* _____ down for a nap.

18. Mark Pajak, who is 84 years old, has *(run)* _____ four miles every day since he was 18 years old.

Irregular Verbs 2

Practice using irregular verbs. Try to memorize the forms of the most common ones. Turn to 720.2 in *Write Source*.

> **Circle** the correct verb form in each sentence.

1. He has (*wrote,* (*written*)) and published several short mystery stories.

2. She has (*growed, grown*) Jerusalem artichokes.

3. The choir has (*sang, sung*) every song in their repertoire.

4. We (*hide, hid*) her present, but she found it anyway.

5. The horses (*lead, led*) us to water, and we drank.

6. I (*choose, choosed*) to exercise daily because that helps me stay fit.

7. She is afraid of dogs because she has been (*bit, bitten*) several times.

> **Tell** whether the verbs below are present tense, past tense, or past participle. (Some verbs can be more than one tense.)

1. dragged _past tense/ past participle_
2. spoken _____
3. rose _____
4. dived _____
5. catch _____
6. drunk _____
7. begin _____
8. swum _____
9. write _____
10. chosen _____
11. stolen _____
12. slew _____
13. shrank _____
14. lied _____
15. come _____
16. set _____
17. given _____
18. swam _____
19. shine _____
20. lead _____

Extend: Review the chart at 720.2 in *Write Source* and make a list of the irregular verbs that trouble you. Refer to your list whenever you proofread your writing.

Troublesome Verbs

It is not unusual to have trouble using certain verbs correctly (for example, *lay/lie, accept/except*). This exercise will offer practice in this area. Turn to pages 676–696 in *Write Source*.

> **Circle** the correct verbs in the following sentences.

1. Roné, why don't you (*lay*, *lie*) the mat on the grass?

2. I think I will (*set*, *sit*) on this stump to watch the squirrels.

3. Not getting enough sleep (*affects*, *effects*) me negatively.

4. No late assignments will be (*accepted*, *excepted*).

5. The dog often (*lays*, *lies*) on the sun-warmed bricks of the patio.

6. Chef Renaud prepared a dessert that (*complemented*, *complimented*) the dinner.

7. Swimming regularly will (*affect*, *effect*) a noticeable change in your muscle tone.

8. At first it felt strange to (*lay*, *lie*) in the hammock, but he (*laid*, *lay*) there all afternoon.

9. Michael Caine (*accepted*, *excepted*) his Oscar with a gracious speech.

10. Her glasses must have been damaged when she (*laid*, *lay*) them on the radiator.

11. You can (*set*, *sit*) the dishes on the counter for now.

12. The plastic bag of garbage had (*laid*, *lain*) in the street for days before someone finally picked it up.

13. Please (*lay*, *lie*) the baby in the crib.

14. Yesterday, I (*lay*, *laid*) down for a nap.

15. He (*lay*, *laid*) the newspaper down before he spoke.

16. (*Sit*, *Set*) here.

17. The committee (*complemented*, *complimented*) Maurice for his efforts.

Extend: Write a sentence for each of the following verbs: *adapt, counsel, desert, infer, heal,* and *lead.*

Review: Verbs 2

Write a short sentence using each verb below in the form requested.

1. fly *(transitive)*: ___Fly the kite carefully._____

2. fly *(intransitive)*: _____

3. appears *(intransitive)*: _____

4. watched *(transitive)*: _____

5. hope *(intransitive)*: _____

Identify each of the underlined verbals as a gerund *(G)*, a participle *(P)*, or an infinitive *(I)*.

1. "An <u>advertising</u> agency is 85 percent confusion and 15 percent commission."

—Fred Allen

2. "Vision is the art of <u>seeing</u> the invisible."   —Jonathan Swift

3. "It is dangerous <u>to be</u> right in matters on which the established authorities are wrong."

—Voltaire

Fill in the blanks with the correct verb tenses.

	Present Tense	Past Tense	Past Participle
1.	swing	swung	swung
2.		laid	
3.	lie (recline)		
4.			swum
5.		went	
6.	lead		

Pretest: Adjectives & Adverbs

> **Decide** whether the blank in each sentence requires an adjective (*ADJ*) or an adverb (*ADV*). Then write an appropriate word in the sentence.

ADV **1.** At a poetry slam, poets recite or perform their works on stage, competing _____*aggressively*_____ to earn the most points.

_____ **2.** These public forums encourage poets to write _____ and share their feelings with an audience.

_____ **3.** Slam poetry is as much about performing _____ as it is about the actual words on the page.

_____ **4.** National slam poetry contests began in 1990 in Chicago and have become _____ popular events throughout the country.

_____ **5.** The audiences at these events are not necessarily _____, refined groups; they cheer wildly on occasion.

_____ **6.** Five judges, _____ selected from the audience, hold up numerical scores after each performance.

_____ **7.** The _____ and _____ scores are thrown out, and the sum of the middle three is the person's score.

_____ **8.** Slam poetry is a national grassroots movement that has become very _____ .

_____ **9.** William Shakespeare may be the _____ poet of all time, but he is very difficult for some modern readers to understand.

_____ **10.** Shakespeare probably would not think _____ of today's poetry slams; in fact, he probably would enjoy them.

Adjectives (Articles)

An adjective describes a noun or a pronoun. Articles (*a, an, the*) are a special group of adjectives. Turn to page 728 in *Write Source*.

> **Underline** the adjectives, including articles in the following passage.

1   So you saw <u>a</u> <u>scary</u> film and never want to go into a thick forest again. But,

2   let's say that you *are*, unfortunately, stranded in a remote wilderness area. Let's

3   say you wandered off the marked trail and find yourself lost. Here's your first

4   piece of advice: Stop where you are!

5   Second, take stock of the situation. Let's say you have a sturdy backpack

6   with an extra set of warm clothes, some dry matches, a nondigital wristwatch,

7   and a pop-up tent. But you've lost your map and compass. What do you do?

8   If you are in bright sunlight, you can follow these simple instructions to

9   make a crude compass. Push a thin stick (or even an ordinary pencil) into the

10   ground. Hold your trusty nondigital watch flat, with the face toward the sky.

11   Position the watch so that the shadow from the stick falls exactly over the hour

12   hand. Here's what your crude compass will tell you: The halfway point between

13   the 12 on the watch and the hour hand points south.

14   Try to get your bearings and remember when—and where—you became

15   lost. If you are in safe and easy terrain, you could retrace your steps. Hike in the

16   direction that you came from and look for any tracks you may have left behind.

17   If you've been lost for 10 minutes, hike back 10 minutes to find the trail. If you

18   can't find the trail (or any trail), go back to your starting point and try again.

19   Look near rivers and streams for usable paths. As you wander, mark your path

20   with small piles of rocks or sticks. If you can't find a way out easily, stay and

21   wait for rescue. Even if it's daytime, a smoky fire makes a good signal.

Forms of Adjectives

Adjectives have three forms: *positive* (for describing one subject), *comparative* (for comparing two people or things), and *superlative* (for comparing three or more people or things). Turn to 728.2 in *Write Source*.

Write in the adjective of your choice using the form indicated in the sentences below.

1. Even though cats and dogs come from the same ancestor, their behavior is very

____**different**____ (*positive*).

2. A cat uses its _____ (*positive*) tail to balance itself when it

jumps. A dog wags its tail to show happiness.

3. A cat chases _____ (*positive*) mice, while a dog chases cats.

4. Therefore, one would assume that the dog is the _____

(*superlative*) of the three.

5. A dog will usually come when called, while a cat will usually ignore you. This

shows that a dog is _____ (*comparative*) than a cat.

6. Cats and cat owners are often seen as being _____ (*comparative*)

than dogs and dog owners.

7. When fetching a ball, a stick, or a disk, a dog plays until it is _____

(*positive*). A cat plays only when it is in a _____ (*positive*) mood.

8. Both dogs and cats have a _____ (*comparative*) sense of smell

than humans have.

9. A dog has 200 million smell cells in its _____ (*positive*) nose. A

human has only 5 million.

10. Pit bulls and Doberman pinschers are _____ (*comparative*) than

Chihuahuas and Yorkshire terriers, but the Irish wolfhound is one of the

_____ (*superlative*) breeds known.

Effective Adjectives

Don't make your reader wade through a string of adjectives to find a noun buried at the end. Instead, choose adjectives carefully, and vary their positions. Professional writers often place adjectives *after* a noun. Study the following sentence from *A Day No Pigs Would Die* by Robert Newton Peck: "I could smell Mama, **crisp** and **starched,** plumping my pillow." The words used as adjectives are boldfaced.

> **Rewrite** the following sentences. Place some or all of the adjectives after the noun to strengthen the focus of the adjectives. Work thoughtfully and ask, "Which adjectives do I want to move?"

1. Then I saw his stern, cold, stony face appear at the door.

Then I saw his stern face, cold and stony, appear at the door.

2. Her sad, bottomless, and utterly vacant eyes will haunt me always.

_____

_____

3. The clear, polished, rhythmical prose resembled poetry.

_____

_____

4. The green, lush, magical fields shimmered in the sunlight.

_____

_____

5. We wept when we saw the heroic, magnificent, futile charge end in disaster.

_____

_____

6. I stopped when I heard the piercing, inhuman, high-pitched scream.

_____

_____

Extend: Write five sentences using two or three adjectives before the noun. Then rewrite the sentences, placing some of the adjectives after the noun. Read several of your before-and-after sentences to a classmate. Talk about the placement of the adjectives.

Review: Adjectives

Fill in the blanks in the sentences below with adjectives. Use vivid, creative adjectives as often as possible, and don't use the same adjective twice.

1. My ___*eccentric*___ Uncle Matt does some really _____ things.

2. When he was a kid, he liked to swim in the _____ quarry!

3. In college, he studied _____ books about _____ subjects.

4. His first job was with an _____ company that sold _____ equipment.

5. Last summer he jumped from a _____ helicopter into the ocean—to study _____ sharks.

6. His apartment is filled with _____ photographs signed by all sorts of _____ people.

7. Uncle Matt is the only person I know who has seen a _____ squid.

8. These days he makes money writing articles filled with his _____ stories.

9. My mom says her brother's life is _____ , but I think it's _____ .

Supply the missing adjectives on the lines below.

Positive	Comparative	Superlative
1. *funny*	funnier	*funniest*
2. smooth		
3.	stranger	
4.		(least) most helpful
5. incredible		

Adverbs

An adverb modifies a verb, an adjective, or another adverb. Adverbs tell *how, when, where, why, how often,* and *how much.* Study the information on page 730 in *Write Source* about using adverbs.

> **Underline** the adverbs in the following sentences.

1. <u>Yesterday</u> it rained heavily, right in the middle of our annual band picnic.

2. As the first drops fell, students and teachers looked nervously at the sky.

3. The light spattering suddenly exploded into an incredible downpour.

4. Teachers stood slowly as the rain pelted down.

5. Students reacted more quickly than the teachers did and ran back to the school building.

6. The teachers hesitated briefly and then joined what had become a mad rush to escape getting totally drenched.

7. The cooks reacted the most quickly of all and instinctively threw plastic bags over the food.

8. Umbrellas were hastily opened for the people grilling hot dogs.

9. Picnic food is always good, but this year it tasted even better than any other year.

10. Inside, some students raced energetically to the cafeteria, while others milled noisily in the halls.

11. Throughout the afternoon, students sat stiffly in soggy clothes while equally damp teachers squished through the day's lessons.

12. Some students wisely suggested that next year's picnic be held in the newly constructed pavilion downtown in the city park.

Extend: Write a paragraph describing an event at your school or home that turned into a near disaster such as the picnic in the exercise above. Trade paragraphs with a classmate and identify the adverbs in one another's work.

Conjunctive Adverbs

Conjunctive adverbs, with the proper punctuation, can be used to combine sentences. Turn to 618.2 in *Write Source* for information.

> **Use** a conjunctive adverb from the list below to combine each pair of sentences. Don't use the same conjunctive adverb twice and don't forget to punctuate correctly.

accordingly	conversely	incidentally	moreover	similarly	then
also	finally	instead	nevertheless	specifically	therefore
besides	furthermore	likewise	nonetheless	still	thus
consequently	however	meanwhile	otherwise	subsequently	

1. There have been many popular rock groups. Most groups last only a short time.

There have been many popular rock groups; still, most groups

last only a short time.

2. Many groups would like to try new styles. They follow the wishes of their fans for the same "signature sound" on each new recording.

3. Record companies are hesitant to tamper with a winning format. Groups fall into the rut of imitating their earlier successes.

4. Trends in music constantly change. New groups emerge to displace the old ones.

5. The audience for most rock groups is largely young people. The Rolling Stones attract huge crowds of older fans.

Extend: Write a paragraph describing your feelings about a particular type of music or a musician. Include at least three sentences using conjunctive adverbs.

Forms of Adverbs

Like adjectives, adverbs have three forms: *positive* (for describing one subject), *comparative* (for comparing two people or things), and *superlative* (for comparing three or more people or things). Turn to 730.2 in *Write Source*.

> **Read** the sentences below. Then rewrite each adverb as directed. Some sentences will need to be slightly modified.

1. *Positive:* My dad snores loudly.

2. *Comparative:* __My dad snores louder than my mom snores.__

3. *Superlative:* My sister snores the loudest of anyone in our family.

4. *Positive:* _____

5. *Comparative:* _____

6. *Superlative:* The third horse to compete jumped best of all.

7. *Positive:* NASCAR racers drive fast.

8. *Comparative:* _____

9. *Superlative:* _____

10. *Positive:* _____

11. *Comparative:* Tina stepped more lightly than Ed over the broken glass.

12. *Superlative:* _____

13. *Positive:* _____

14. *Comparative:* His computer processes more slowly than ours does.

15. *Superlative:* _____

Extend: Write three sentences, each with a different positive, comparative, or superlative adverb. Then trade papers with a classmate and write new sentences like those in the exercise above.

Using Adverbs vs. Alternatives

Specific adverbs can add power and meaning to vague or weak verbs. Sometimes, however, a stronger verb is a better choice altogether. Turn to page 245 in *Write Source*.

Replace the underlined verb + adverb combinations in the sentences below with single, more descriptive verbs. You may refer to a thesaurus for help.

1. The massive lineman intercepted the ball and <u>ran clumsily</u> into the end zone.

lumbered   *plodded*   *lurched*

2. The quarterback <u>quickly threw</u> the ball to the tailback.

_____   _____   _____

3. Susan <u>ran quickly</u> to catch the bus.

_____   _____   _____

4. The soldier <u>walked heavily</u> through the ankle-deep mud.

_____   _____   _____

5. The winning fighter <u>ran happily</u> around the ring.

_____   _____   _____

6. The loser <u>sat tiredly</u> in his corner.

_____   _____   _____

7. Angela <u>wearily carried</u> her book bag off the bus.

_____   _____   _____

8. The exhausted runner <u>ran haltingly</u> toward the finish line.

_____   _____   _____

9. The audience applauded as the politician <u>moved confidently</u> to the podium.

_____   _____   _____

10. The sun <u>shone brightly</u> through the window.

_____   _____   _____

Extend: List five specific verbs that could be used in place of "said."

Review: Adverbs

> **Underline** the adverbs in the following sentences. Write **P** for positive, **C** for comparative, or **S** for superlative above each. Circle the conjunctive adverbs.

1. The Taj Mahal is an impressive monument located in Agra, India;(furthermore,) it is one of the world's most magnificently designed and engineered buildings. *(S above "most magnificently")*

2. It was originally designed by a Turkish architect and gradually constructed between 1632 and 1648.

3. The Taj Mahal was built as a monument to eternally commemorate the love between Shah Jahan and his second wife, Mumtaz-i-Mahal.

4. Mumtaz was his constant companion; moreover, she served better than anyone else as his counselor and conscience.

5. She quietly inspired the shah to become more generously inclined toward his subjects, earning Mumtaz the unquestioned loyalty of the Indian people.

6. Most amazingly, Mumtaz gave birth to 14 children.

7. Her early death resulted from the particularly difficult and painful birth of her last child.

8. Shah Jahan immediately ordered the finest tomb to be built, but it took nearly 17 years to complete.

9. The tomb chamber is lit naturally by sunlight passing through the most intricately carved screens.

10. "Taj Mahal" most commonly translates to "Crown of the Palace"; however, it is more generally believed to be the abbreviated name of Mumtaz-i-Mahal.

Pretest: Prepositions, Conjunctions, & Interjections

> **Circle** the interjections and draw two lines under all the conjunctions in the following sentences.

1. (Okay,) either I learn a few things about chemistry, or I will be in big trouble.

2. Lead, mercury, gold, silver, copper, and sulfur were all discovered by early humans, and hydrogen, helium, nitrogen, and oxygen were discovered later.

3. Imagine, oxygen wasn't discovered until 1774, yet it is one of the most common elements on the planet.

4. Most people probably think oxygen is the most common element in the earth's atmosphere, but, *au contraire*, nitrogen is.

5. When common elements are joined together, they form compounds like water and salt.

> **Underline** the prepositional phrases in the following sentences. Write **P** above the prepositions and write **O** above the objects of the prepositions.

1. Water is a compound of hydrogen and oxygen, and salt is a compound of sodium and chlorine.

2. Both diamonds and graphite are forms of carbon.

3. Only 91 of the 112 elements occur naturally on or in the ground.

4. Though metals can be mined from the earth, it makes sense from an ecological standpoint to recycle metals whenever possible.

5. Everything that we see and use is made of elements, so you can honestly say the answer to every question ever asked in science class is, "It's elemental."

6. You may, however, need a better variety of answers than that if you want to get a passing grade in the class.

Prepositions & Interjections

A *preposition* is a word (or group of words) that shows the relationship between its object and another word in the sentence. An *interjection* is a word or an expression that communicates strong emotion or surprise. Turn to pages 732 and 734 in *Write Source*.

> **Identify** each word below as either a preposition or an interjection. Then write a sentence using the word.

1. among ___(preposition) We were among the first to arrive.___

2. before _____

_____

3. yipes _____

_____

4. through _____

_____

5. wow _____

_____

6. away from _____

_____

7. hooray _____

_____

8. my goodness _____

_____

9. in addition to _____

_____

10. oh, no _____

_____

Coordinating Conjunctions

Coordinating conjunctions connect a word to a word, a phrase to a phrase, or a clause to a clause when these are equal or of the same type. Turn to 734.1 in *Write Source*.

> **Underline** the coordinating conjunctions in the following sentences. Then write your own sentences modeling those below and using the same coordinating conjunctions.

1. Picking up a pad <u>and</u> grabbing a pencil, Andrei was ready to take a message.

Pulling on her boots and taking her walking stick, Grandma went to get her

mail.

2. He would not wear galoshes nor use an umbrella.

_____

_____

3. Joaquin always used brown paper bags or the comics to wrap gifts.

_____

_____

4. Hesitant to join the club but wanting to fit in, Leon had a decision to make.

_____

_____

5. She had a feeling she wasn't doing it right, for she didn't have a clue as to the proper procedure.

_____

_____

6. Assertive yet sensitive—that's a good combination of leadership qualities.

_____

7. Anita never learned how to drive, so she took the bus everywhere.

_____

_____

Correlative & Subordinating Conjunctions

Correlative conjunctions are conjunctions used in pairs such as *either, or* and *neither, nor*. Subordinating conjunctions such as *after, before,* or *because* connect and show the relationship between two clauses that are not equally important. Turn to 734.2–734.3 in *Write Source*.

> **Complete** sentences 2–6 below with clauses that include the conjunctions given. (Be careful not to write prepositional phrases instead; some of these conjunctions can also be prepositions.) Complete sentences 7–8 with phrases that include the conjunctions given.

1. *(before)* Samantha raised her hand ___before she heard the whole question___ .

2. *(although)* My brother is usually on time, _____ .

    _____

3. *(unless)* We will all go hiking next weekend _____ .

    _____

4. *(as long as)* _____

    _____ , you'll be a safe driver.

5. *(after)* _____

    _____ , I bought myself a new alarm clock.

6. *(while)* _____

    _____ , I finished painting the clock.

7. *(both, and)* _____

    _____ are dirty.

8. *(not only, but also)* _____

    _____ wickedly windy.

Extend: Write sentences that include the following subordinating conjunctions: *because, if,* and *since.*

Review: Prepositions, Conjunctions, & Interjections

> **Underline** and label each interjection *(I)* and each conjunction *(C)* below. Circle each prepositional phrase and label the preposition *(P)* and the object *(O)*.

1. "Bah humbug!" said Scrooge as he peered over his large and cluttered desk.

2. Because Elaine has chicken pox, she can attend neither the concert nor the party.

3. As she rounded the corner, the policewoman saw the suspect—just before he jumped on the bus and rode away.

4. Holy smokes! The ball not only went over the fence but also out of the park!

5. The president assured his stockholders that the company would continue to grow, provided that the scandal concerning the lawsuits did not grow.

6. We can all go to the concert, but someone has to sit on the lawn.

7. "Either take your sister skating," Mom said, "or come to the laundromat with me."

8. Dad had a dog of his own when he was young, so I want to have one, too.

> **List** each conjunction from the sentences above in the appropriate column below.

Coordinating	Correlative	Subordinating
		as

Review: Parts of Speech

> **Identify** each underlined word or phrase in the following paragraph in the blanks on the next page. Name the part of speech or verbal each word or phrase represents; also, tell how each functions in the sentence. (*For example:* "Dad" is a noun used as a subject.)

My dad¹ and I argue² about music³ all the time. Dad likes classic rock, folk music, jazz, and some classical music. I stick pretty much with current⁴ rock groups, although I like some Beatles material, and I sometimes⁵ listen to the Rolling Stones. My dad is also a big fan⁶ of Kris Kristofferson, the country-and-western singer. I can enjoy some of my father's music, but⁷ I draw the line at Kristofferson. Hearing⁸ Kristofferson trying to sing is⁹ painful to me. He¹⁰ mumbles.¹¹ When I complain, Dad always¹² tells me I should listen because Kristofferson is a better¹³ songwriter than singer. Kristofferson's¹⁴ singing seems so bad that anything else must be better. Wow,¹⁵ that doesn't say much for his¹⁶ singing. Dad says Kristofferson was a Rhodes scholar. That¹⁷ seems unusual¹⁸ for a country-and-western singer. Maybe¹⁹ I'll listen a little more closely the next time Dad plays Kristofferson's songs. In the meantime, I'll²⁰ stick with Black Eyed Peas.

1. *"Dad"* is a noun used as the subject of the sentence.

2. *"Argue"*

3. *"Music"*

4. *"Current"*

5. *"Sometimes"*

6. *"Fan"*

7. *"But"*

8. *"Hearing"*

9. *"Is"*

10. *"He"*

11. *"Mumbles"*

12. *"Always"*

13. *"Better"*

14. *"Kristofferson's"*

15. *"Wow"*

16. *"His"*

17. *"That"*

18. *"Unusual"*

19. *"Maybe"*

20. *"I'll"*

Sentence Activities

The activities in this section cover three important areas: (1) the basic parts, types, and kinds of sentences as well as agreement issues; (2) methods for writing smooth-reading sentences; and (3) common sentence errors. Most activities include practice in which you review, combine, or analyze different sentences. In addition, the Extend activities provide follow-up practice with certain skills.

Pretest: Subjects & Predicates

Draw a vertical line between the complete subject and the complete predicate in the following sentences. Then underline the simple or compound subject once and the simple or compound predicate twice.

1. Ten legal <u>holidays</u> | <u><u>are observed</u></u> in the United States.

2. Columbus Day, Martin Luther King, Jr.'s, birthday, and Veterans Day are three such holidays.

3. International businesses need to keep track of all the legal holidays in all the countries of the world.

4. It is quite a nightmare!

5. Paul Spraos, a London-born entrepreneur, recognized the problem all these holidays posed for businesses.

6. He decided to create a perpetual global calendar.

7. Muslim holidays, for example, are determined by the phase of the moon and vary from one Muslim country to the next.

8. Weekends are not easy to calculate either.

9. A weekend means every Sunday and every second and fourth Saturday in Taiwan.

10. Weekends include every Sunday and the first Saturday of each month in Malaysia.

11. Lithuanians occasionally observe a one-day weekend followed by a four-day weekend.

12. Failing to pay or to collect large interest payments on holidays around the world, businesses and banks lose or gain millions of dollars.

13. Many businesses rely on Mr. Spraos' perpetual global calendar.

Subjects & Predicates

A sentence has a subject (usually a noun or a pronoun) and a predicate (verb). The subject is the part of the sentence about which something is said. The predicate is the part of the sentence that shows action or says something about the subject. Turn to pages 738 and 740 in *Write Source*.

> **Draw** one line under the complete subject and two lines under the complete predicate in the following sentences. Circle the simple subject and simple predicate. (There is one compound sentence—it will have two subjects and two predicates. Also, two sentences have compound verbs.)

1. With the flavor of ham and biscuit still in his mouth, the (boy) (felt) good.

—William H. Armstrong, *Sounder*

2. He kept the other key, the one to the padlock on the bear's neck.

—Hal Borland, *When the Legends Die*

3. In a kind of furious daze, forgetting the eggs, I got a big old gray peach basket off the porch and dragged it down the path.

—Olive Ann Burns, *Cold Sassy Tree*

4. I looked out across the ravaged fields and saw Romey, a vaporous figure in the distance, moving around in Roy Luther's garden.

—Vera and Bill Cleaver, *Where the Lilies Bloom*

5. The wheels struck the runway and the plane pulled up by a small wooden house on the tundra, the terminal building.

—Jean Craighead George, *Julie of the Wolves*

6. We have confused the free with the free and easy.

—Adlai Stevenson, *Wall Street Journal*

7. The ride ended too quickly, in front of a large, shabby building.

—Robert Lipsyte, *The Contender*

Extend: Write down what you know about subjects and predicates. Write to a certain audience: a young child, someone learning English, your teacher, or a friend.

Review: Subjects & Predicates

> **Write** sentences using the words listed as your subjects and predicates.

1. Compound subject: *Sonja and Brian;* Predicate: *swim*

Sonja and Brian swim in the creek, the one that flows through the

Bartleson's meadow.

2. Subject: *name of your school;* Predicate: *displays*

_____

_____

3. Subject: *turnips;* Predicate: *are*

_____

_____

4. Subject: *elephants;* Predicate: *parade*

_____

_____

5. Compound subject: *eggs and bacon;* Compound predicate: *sizzle and crackle*

_____

_____

6. Subject: *darkness;* Predicate: *scares*

_____

_____

7. Subject: *your choice;* Predicate: *your choice*

_____

_____

Pretest: Phrases

Identify the underlined phrases using **G** for gerund, **I** for infinitive, **P** for participial, and **A** for appositive. Circle the prepositional phrases. (*Remember:* a prepositional phrase is often part of another kind of phrase.) Study the first sentence to see how to mark such constructions.

1. Morse code was one (of the greatest inventions) (of the nineteenth century.)

2. Morse code made it possible to send messages across long distances.

3. For the first time in the history of the world, people could send messages

quickly.

4. Morse code, a system of dots and dashes, stands for letters of the alphabet and

for numerals.

5. On May 24, 1844, Samuel Morse, the inventor of the Morse code, sent the first

telegraphic message, saying "What hath God wrought!"

Underline and identify the phrases in the following sentences. Use the same symbols as above and circle the prepositional phrases.

        G

1. Learning Morse code requires many months (of study.)

2. Sending or receiving Morse code messages at an acceptable rate of speed takes

years to learn well.

3. Having learned the Morse code, people feel great pride in their skill.

4. Morse code, a remarkable system of dots and dashes, is not taught

to many people nowadays.

5. For better or for worse, the Morse code is being replaced by the Internet and

fax machines.

Verbal Phrases

A verbal is a word that is derived from a verb but acts as another part of speech. There are three kinds of verbals: gerunds, infinitives, and participles. See the chart below.

Type of Verbal	Used as		
	Noun	**Adjective**	**Adverb**
Gerund (ends in *-ing*)	X		
Infinitive (introduced by *to*)	X	X	X
Participle (often ends in *-ing* or *-ed*)		X	

A verbal phrase contains a verbal and all of its complements and modifiers. The whole phrase then functions as a noun, an adjective, or an adverb. Turn to page 726 in *Write Source*.

Identify the underlined verbal phrases in the following sentences. Write *G* for gerund, *I* for infinitive, and *P* for participial. Also label each infinitive as either *N* for noun, *ADJ* for adjective, or *ADV* for adverb.

_____*I, ADJ*_____ **1.** Most sports cars have low, aerodynamic bodies <u>to cut through the air easily</u>.

_____ **2.** A sports car is an automobile <u>designed for performance</u>.

_____ **3.** <u>Weighing less than other cars</u> gives a sports car improved engine performance.

_____ **4.** Low weight also makes it easier <u>to slow down and turn corners</u>.

_____ **5.** <u>To turn corners faster</u>, the cars need a firm grip on the road.

_____ **6.** Sports cars have wide tires and a firm suspension, <u>enabling better handling</u>.

_____ **7.** <u>Producing limited quantities</u> drives up the cost of these vehicles.

_____ **8.** <u>To own an expensive sports car</u> is a status symbol for some people.

_____ **9.** I would love <u>driving a sports car</u>.

_____ **10.** <u>Zooming around the countryside</u>, I'd loudly sing my favorite songs!

Extend: Write three sentences about a hobby. Each sentence should use a different type of verbal phrase.

Prepositional & Appositive Phrases

A prepositional phrase consists of a preposition, its object, and any modifiers. Turn to page 742 and page 744 in *Write Source*. An appositive phrase consists of a noun and its modifiers and follows the noun or pronoun it renames. Turn to 742.1 in *Write Source*.

> **Underline** the prepositional and appositive phrases below. Circle each preposition and connect it to its object with an arrow.

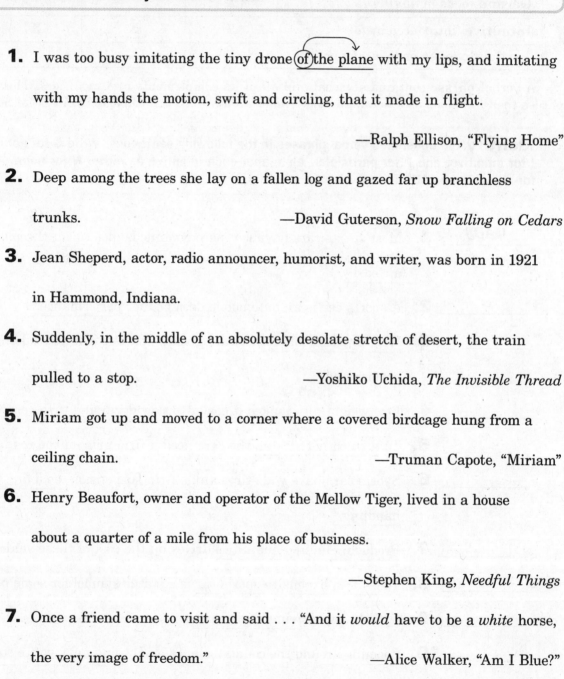

1. I was too busy imitating the tiny drone of the plane with my lips, and imitating

with my hands the motion, swift and circling, that it made in flight.

—Ralph Ellison, "Flying Home"

2. Deep among the trees she lay on a fallen log and gazed far up branchless

trunks. —David Guterson, *Snow Falling on Cedars*

3. Jean Sheperd, actor, radio announcer, humorist, and writer, was born in 1921

in Hammond, Indiana.

4. Suddenly, in the middle of an absolutely desolate stretch of desert, the train

pulled to a stop. —Yoshiko Uchida, *The Invisible Thread*

5. Miriam got up and moved to a corner where a covered birdcage hung from a

ceiling chain. —Truman Capote, "Miriam"

6. Henry Beaufort, owner and operator of the Mellow Tiger, lived in a house

about a quarter of a mile from his place of business.

—Stephen King, *Needful Things*

7. Once a friend came to visit and said . . . "And it *would* have to be a *white* horse,

the very image of freedom." —Alice Walker, "Am I Blue?"

Extend: Write three to five sentences using appositives to describe people you know. Try to include at least one prepositional phrase in each sentence.

Absolute Phrases

Many absolute phrases begin with a possessive pronoun: *my, his, her, its, our, their.* (Many absolute phrases also fit this pattern: If you insert *was* or *were* right after the subject in an absolute phrase, the phrase turns into a sentence.) Turn to page 744 in *Write Source.*

 Makem, *his eyes shining with delight,* climbed into a seat on the Ferris wheel. (If you add *were* to the absolute phrase, it turns into a sentence: *His eyes were shining with delight.*)

Underline the absolute phrases in the following sentences.

1. Mrs. O'Tooles' flowers, their colors so vibrant, make her backyard irresistible to

the eye.

2. Mrs. O'Tooles, her pruning shears in hand, trimmed her beautiful rose bushes.

3. My favorite flowers are her day lilies and tiger lilies, their blossoms signaling

summer to me.

Model the following sentences by professional writers to learn how to write your own absolutes. The absolute phrases have been underlined.

1. Her choosing done, her house neat, she went outside and sat on the step again.
                                                    —Hal Borland, *When the Legends Die*

Her decision made, her bags packed, Myrtle walked downstairs and waited

at the curb.

2. Calvin, his face screwed up with grim determination, his mouth scowling, did not
relax his hold.   —Madeleine L'Engle, *A Wrinkle in Time*

_____

_____

3. Little Man flashed proudly past, his face and hands clean and his black shoes
shining again.   —Mildred D. Taylor, *Roll of Thunder, Hear My Cry*

_____

_____

© Houghton Mifflin Harcourt Publishing Company

Effective Phrases

Using phrases well gives writing a professional quality. Turn to page 742 in *Write Source*.

> **Imitate** the following sentences written by well-known authors. Underline your phrases.

1. *(one gerund and one prepositional phrase)* My whole body would assume regular movements; my shoveling would be described by identical, even movements.
—Richard Rodriguez, "Los Pobres"

<u>My long fingers would shove the piano keys;</u> my playing would be defined by

low, mournful chords.

2. *(one participial, five prepositional, and two appositive phrases)* I squinted, pressing my face close to the window, and saw Baptiste, my friend from the old days at the shop, a friend from the times of long ago.
—Robert Cormier, *Take Me Where the Good Times Are*

_____

_____

_____

_____

3. *(three infinitive phrases)* Brother Coyote can't help himself; he likes man—maybe not to talk to or [to] play with, but definitely to live next door to.
—Michelle Huneven, "Living Well Is the Best Revenge— Just Ask the Urban Coyote"

_____

_____

_____

4. *(two absolute phrases)* She was not the small freckle-faced Jenny that I had known . . . but a lovely sweet sixteen . . . her nails polished and her dark hair scented.
—Christy Brown, *My Left Foot*

_____

_____

_____

_____

Review: Phrases

> **Label** each of the phrases enclosed in parentheses below: use **G** for gerund, **I** for infinitive, **P** for participial, **A** for appositive, and **AB** for absolute. Then underline all prepositional phrases. *Remember:* Some phrases contain another phrase (usually a prepositional phrase).

1. Cars (owned *P* by people in large cities), (large as in New York or Paris) *A*, are apt (to cause the owner stress) *I*.

2. A person can drive for hours without (finding a place) (to park).

3. Drivers, (frustrated beyond reason), are always on edge.

4. (Their horns blaring loudly), dozens of yellow cabs (driven by professional drivers) muscle their way down the street.

5. It takes a genius (to decipher the parking signs).

6. Traffic police (armed with blank citation books) patrol the streets.

7. (Getting a traffic ticket) means a hefty fine or possibly a court date.

8. Many drivers, (tired of complicated parking restrictions, daily gridlock, and other drivers' bad tempers), decide (to travel by bus or subway).

9. Many big-city car owners choose (to pay two or three hundred dollars a month for a parking space in their building's lot).

10. For many drivers, the negatives of (driving a car) far outweigh any advantages a car might provide.

11. When you don't own a car, neighborhood grocery stores—(aisles packed with people and products), (customers waiting forever in lines)—are the only places (to buy groceries).

12. (Owning a car in a big city), whether you use it or not, can be expensive and stressful.

Pretest: Clauses

> **Identify** each underlined clause as *I* for independent or *D* for dependent. If the clause is dependent, write adjective, adverb, or noun in the blank.

         I

_____ **1.** For the most part, <u>a sport is a localized event.</u>

_____ **2.** Students at Central High think everyone wants to hear about their team, <u>but students at South High do not agree.</u>

_____ **3.** A person who travels to different parts of the country will soon see <u>that his or her favorite team rates only a two-line comment.</u>

_____ **4.** Not long ago, <u>I looked for and couldn't even find an article on my favorite team,</u> <u>which is in another state.</u>

_____ **5.** The newspaper ignored my team, which had completely dominated the visiting team, <u>while printing six pages devoted to the big team in this state.</u>

_____ **6.** <u>Most people don't want to read about another team,</u> even if it is the best team in the world.

_____ **7.** The term "world champions" does not mean a thing to millions of people <u>who don't know about those champions.</u>

_____ **8.** Sports are exciting <u>when life is going well.</u>

_____ **9.** In reality, sports <u>which provide entertainment for many people</u> don't make a difference in important life issues.

_____ **10.** This doesn't mean you shouldn't get caught up in a game, but it does mean <u>that you should keep sports in perspective.</u>

Independent & Dependent Clauses

An independent clause presents a complete thought and can stand alone as a sentence. A dependent clause does not present a complete thought and cannot stand alone as a sentence. The three types of dependent clauses are the adverb clause, the adjective clause, and the noun clause. Turn to 744.1–744.2 in *Write Source*.

> **Finish** the following sentences by completing the dependent clause using the given conjunction or relative pronoun. Then identify the dependent clause by writing adverb, adjective, or noun in brackets.

1. Sylvia will travel to Spain next summer, unless _she is unable to save_

enough money. [adverb]

2. Although _____

_____ , he already excelled at the violin.

3. My Uncle Howard, who _____

_____ , will retire next month.

4. I wish I could remember where _____

_____

5. Since _____

_____ , I decided to wear a blue dress to the dance.

6. Saturday's game, which _____ ,

will be held rain or shine.

7. Mother said that _____

8. The new mayor, whose _____

_____ , wants to build three new schools.

9. As long as _____

_____ , we will have a great time in Florida.

10. The rain that _____ ruined our picnic.

Extend: Write three complex sentences about an acquaintance. Your sentences should include one of each of the three types of dependent clauses.

Adverb Clauses

An adverb clause is a type of dependent clause that modifies a verb, an adjective, or an adverb. Adverb clauses often explain *when? where? why?* or *how?* (See the categories listed below.) Adverb clauses always begin with a subordinating conjunction. Turn to 744.2 in *Write Source*.

Category	Subordinating Conjunctions
To show time	before, after, when, until, since, while
To show reasons	because, since
To show purpose	that, so that, in order that
To show conditions	if, unless, although, as long as, though

Write four sentences using adverb clauses; underline the adverb clause. Use a subordinating conjunction from the chart above that matches the category listed in parentheses below.

1. (reasons) _I went straight home after school <u>because I had said I'd fix</u>_

<u>supper for our family.</u>

2. (purpose) _____

_____

_____

3. (conditions) _____

_____

_____

4. (time) _____

_____

_____

5. (reasons) _____

_____

Extend: Choose a piece of your writing. As you read it, draw one line under sentences that could be main ideas and draw two lines under sentences that could be subordinated. Finally, rewrite the selected sentences, combining them appropriately.

Adjective Clauses

An adjective clause is a type of dependent clause that modifies a noun or a pronoun. Most adjective clauses begin with a relative pronoun: *who, whom, whose, which, that.* Turn to 706.2 and 744.2 in *Write Source.* Also see the "who, which, that" entry on page 696.

> **Write** six sentences containing adjective clauses. Use a relative pronoun to create each clause.

1. Create an adjective clause that describes a person.

Tamara, who is a great singer, got the lead role in the musical.

2. Create an adjective clause that refers to a thing.

_____

_____

3. Create an adjective clause that refers to an abstract idea.

_____

_____

4. Use the relative pronoun *whose* to show possession.

_____

_____

5. Create an adjective clause that refers to a place.

_____

_____

6. Create an adjective clause that modifies a pronoun.

_____

_____

7. Use the relative pronoun *that* to indicate a specific thing.

_____

_____

Review: Clauses

Use the word groups listed below as subjects for the sentences you will complete. Include an independent clause and the type of dependent clause indicated for each sentence. Underline your dependent clauses.

1. *(adjective clause)* The friendly police officer, <u>who directs traffic at Krall and Oakburn,</u> pretends he is dancing.

2. *(adjective clause)* A tired young man _____

3. *(adverb clause)* The soccer team _____

4. *(adjective clause)* Her favorite movie _____

5. *(adjective clause)* My hopes and dreams _____

6. *(noun clause)* Next Friday's exam _____

7. *(noun clause)* The flight attendants _____

Pretest: Sentences

_CX_   **1.** Ever since the Pilgrims survived their first harsh winter in the new world, Americans have set aside a day to remember the Pilgrims and to give thanks.

_____   **2.** Do you remember dressing up as Pilgrims or as Native Americans for Thanksgiving plays in elementary school?

_____   **3.** Thanksgiving was celebrated unofficially for many years, but it took three great presidents and one editor of a women's journal to make it an official holiday.

_____   **4.** On October 3, 1789, George Washington issued the first official Thanksgiving proclamation.

_____   **5.** After Washington left office, the idea of a national day of thanksgiving was forgotten for a time; but Sarah Josepha Hale, who was editor of _Godey's Lady's Book_ and the daughter of a Revolutionary War hero, revived the idea during the Civil War.

_____   **6.** Her letter to President Lincoln on September 28, 1863, arrived three months after the battle of Gettysburg, which is considered a turning point in the war, and apparently Lincoln took time to study Hale's request.

_____   **7.** That fall Lincoln proclaimed a day of "thanksgiving and praise" to a country torn apart by war.

_____   **8.** Lincoln's successors celebrated the holiday on the last Thursday of November until 1939, when President Franklin D. Roosevelt moved Thanksgiving back a week.

_____   **9.** Americans were upset; in fact, many were outraged!

_____ **10.** Roosevelt backed off, but shortly after the United States got into World War II, he signed an Act of Congress that permanently placed Thanksgiving on the fourth Thursday of November, where it has been ever since.

Kinds of Sentences

Sentences can make five basic kinds of statements: *declarative, interrogative, imperative, exclamatory,* and *conditional.* Turn to 746.1 in *Write Source.*

> **Write** the kinds of sentences asked for using the subject and verb given. Feel free to change the form or tense of the verbs given to whatever will work best for your sentence.

1. Exclamatory: *I, love*

I love thunderstorms!
_____

2. Imperative: *you, wash*

_____

3. Conditional: *doctor, leave*

_____

4. Interrogative: *dogs, run*

_____

5. Declarative: *volcanoes, erupt*

_____

6. Interrogative: *you, go*

_____

7. Exclamatory: *I, swim*

_____

8. Imperative: *you, remember*

_____

9. Declarative: *Andy, fix*

_____

Extend: Find an example of each kind of sentence in a textbook. If you cannot find a particular example, create one. As you search for your examples, check to see if you could add variety and impact to the writing by using different kinds of sentences.

Simple & Compound Sentences

There are four types of sentences. This exercise concentrates on simple and compound sentences. Turn to 748.1 in *Write Source*.

> **The magician performed many tricks and illusions.**
> (Simple sentences have only one independent clause and no dependent clauses. Even so, they may contain one or more phrases, a single or a compound subject, and a single or a compound predicate.)

> **He sawed his assistant in half, and then he escaped from a straitjacket.**
> (Compound sentences are made up of two independent clauses joined by punctuation, a coordinating conjunction, or both.

Label the following sentences either simple or compound.

---

simple   **1.** Every day fishing boats leave safe harbors to fish the seas.

2. The crews of these boats fish in any weather, and most of them love the adventure.

3. Some of the boats trail huge nets behind them to catch fish.

4. At one time, these nets caught sea mammals as well, but new net designs allow these animals to escape.

5. Fishing boats no longer catch as many fish as possible; in fact, most countries now limit the number of fish taken in a season.

6. Those fishing in northern oceans face the dangers of high seas and icy equipment.

7. Monster waves can overwhelm a boat, and too much ice on board can cause a boat to capsize.

8. Many people regard deep-sea fishing as the most hazardous job in the world.

9. Even so, thousands of men and women make a living on oceans and seas around the world.

10. These people work long hours in dangerous conditions, and we enjoy delicious meals of salmon, flounder, and halibut.

Extend: Select four of the simple sentences above and combine them to create two compound sentences.

Complex & Compound-Complex Sentences

There are four types of sentences. This exercise concentrates on complex and compound-complex sentences. Turn to 748.1 in *Write Source*.

> **I loved to go hiking in the forest when I was younger.**
> (Complex sentences contain one independent clause and one or more dependent clauses.)

> **The forest was always a magical place, and I marveled at the number of creatures that lived in a single acre.**
> (Compound-complex sentences contain two or more independent clauses and one or more dependent clauses.)

Label each of the following sentences. Use **CX** for complex or **CD-CX** for compound-complex.

_CD-CX_ **1.** During the last five years, my friends and I have studied and visited a number of nature preserves, so we think of ourselves as experts who have something to share.

_____ **2.** Here are some of the interesting things that we've learned over the years.

_____ **3.** Fairy rings are formed by an ever-expanding circle of fungi that experts say are dark green or brown.

_____ **4.** Because mangroves have complex root systems, the trees only thrive in very watery conditions, such as wetlands and slow-moving rivers.

_____ **5.** Dandelions are typically hated in the United States, but they are highly desired in some parts of Europe, if you can imagine that.

_____ **6.** Venus's-flytraps capture insects in specially adapted leaves that snap shut on their prey.

_____ **7.** Cacti are tough and covered with sharp spines; they have soft, watery interiors and root systems that allow them to absorb water very efficiently.

_____ **8.** Redwoods, the tallest trees in the world, can live to be 2,500 years old; they grow well in California near the Pacific Ocean, which helps provide the moisture they need.

_____ **9.** Of course, we also learned that a few years of education about nature did not make us experts; nevertheless, we still enjoy sharing what we've learned!

Extend: Add an independent clause to two of the complex sentences above to make them compound-complex.

Sentence Modeling 1

Writers learn how to arrange sentences so they can achieve sentence variety and add details. One way to achieve variety is to put the main clause in different positions—at the beginning, in the middle, or at the end. Turn to 750.1 in *Write Source*.

> **Create** a different arrangement for each of the sentences below, changing words as necessary.

1. Miguel pulled into the crowded parking lot and turned up the car stereo.

Pulling into the crowded parking lot, Miguel turned up the car stereo.

_____

2. Stepping down from the truck, I lost my balance, turning my foot under me as I crumpled to the ground.

_____

_____

3. Dancing on her hind legs and whimpering her hello, my dog welcomes me home.

_____

_____

4. Joey spent her leisure time listening to rock music on the radio in the apartment's tiny dining room that also served as her bedroom.

_____

_____

_____

5. Unable to fly due to an ear infection, Vlad rented a car and drove to his sister's wedding in Georgia.

_____

_____

_____

Extend: Select two of the sentences above and rearrange them in yet a different way.

Writers INC 555.1

Sentence Modeling 2

Writers often experiment with a variety of sentence arrangements. Then they select the arrangement they think is best for the piece they are writing. Turn to 750.1 in *Write Source*.

> **Study** the sentence below. Rewrite the sentence five times following the directions for each new arrangement.

"A stillness hovered in the high air, soft, quiet, peaceful."
—Mildred D. Taylor, *Roll of Thunder, Hear My Cry*

1. Place two of the adjectives (*soft, quiet, peaceful*) before *stillness*.

The soft, quiet stillness hovered in the high, peaceful air.

_____

2. Add two adverbs to describe *hovered* and eliminate all the adjectives.

_____

_____

3. Insert an adjective clause, *that hovered in the air,* in the original sentence and add the verb *was*.

_____

_____

4. Insert a participial phrase, *hovering in the high air,* after *stillness* and add the verb *was*.

_____

_____

5. Now use the participial phrase, *hovering in the high air,* as an introductory word group.

_____

_____

6. Which of your four sentences do you prefer? Why? _____

_____

_____

Sentence Modeling 3

Emphasis can be achieved by putting the most important idea at or near the end of a sentence. Turn to 750.1 in *Write Source*.

> **Study** the following sentences written by well-known authors. Carefully note the emphasis and rhythm each author creates. Write your own sentence modeled on each example below, imitating it part by part.

1. In 1985, American unions' slow decline in membership began to turn around—mostly due to the influx of 70,000 new female members.

> —Barbara Ehrenreich, "The Next Wave"

By 2012, the number of e-businesses will have exploded—owing

to the entrepreneurial spirit of American workers.

2. Since advocates for the homeless claim that homelessness is entirely or primarily caused by a housing shortage, they typically deemphasize the role that disabilities like mental illness, alcoholism, and drug abuse play in the plight of the homeless.

> —Thomas J. Main, "What We Know About the Homeless"

_____

_____

_____

3. "Acid rain," the term for precipitation that contains a high concentration of harmful chemicals, is gradually damaging our environment.

_____

_____

_____

4. I discovered—with the help of some especially sensitive teachers—that through writing one can continually bring new selves into being, each with new responsibilities and difficulties, but also with new possibilities.

> —Barbara Mellix, "From Outside, In"

_____

_____

_____

Review: Sentences

> **Label** each sentence below. Use **S** for simple, **CD** for compound, **CX** for complex, and **CD-CX** for compound-complex.

___*S*___ **1.** The curfew started in London during the reign of King Alfred.

_____ **2.** Wooden houses lined the streets of London, and fire was an ever-present danger.

_____ **3.** An open fire burned in the center of every house or in its largest room.

_____ **4.** When the church bells rang in the evening, it was a signal to "cover the fire."

_____ **5.** "Cover the fire," which was slurred together in London speech, became "curfew," and the name stuck.

_____ **6.** Curfew bells were discontinued when better building practices and better fire-fighting equipment were developed.

_____ **7.** Today, curfews are used to help prevent "people" problems, not "fire" problems.

_____ **8.** When a destructive storm hits, curfews prevent injuries by keeping people off the streets.

_____ **9.** Originally, "curfew" meant "cover fire"; today, it means "stay home" to potential troublemakers.

> **Write** sentences as indicated.

1. Rewrite sentence number 1 so that it is an interrogative sentence.

_____

2. Rewrite sentence number 4 so that it is an imperative sentence.

_____

3. Rewrite sentence number 8 so that it is a conditional sentence.

_____

_____

Pretest: Subject-Verb Agreement

Underline the subject for each set of verbs in the sentences below; then circle the verb that agrees in number with the subject.

1. One <u>day</u> *(is,)* *are)* plenty of time to finish this assignment.

2. The crew of the yacht *America (is, are)* considered one of the best in the world.

3. The cause of his problem (was, were) his bad knees.

4. The media *(was, were)* at both the Republican and Democratic conventions.

5. The counseling staff at the high school *(was, were)* honored for providing students with many new services.

6. The rescue squad, along with several police cars, *(was, were)* at the scene of the accident almost immediately.

7. One of the seven lanes *(do, does)* not have a starting block for the runner.

8. There *(was, were)* many students who favored keeping study halls.

9. *(Is, Are)* either of the girls going on the hayride tonight?

10. Here *(is, are)* the pair of gloves you left at my house yesterday.

11. *(Wasn't, Weren't)* Jen or Gabbie supposed to help clean up this mess?

12. Around the corner *(is, are)* several fresh footprints in the cement.

13. *(Has, Have)* the thunder and lightning stopped yet?

14. There in the distance *(was, were)* the remains of the ghost town.

15. In the gymnasium *(was, were)* the acrobats and their coaches.

16. Looking at the paintings in the gallery *(was, were)* 10 women.

17. Neither Janice nor Liam *(was, were)* going to the tournament.

Subject-Verb Agreement 1

Some nouns that are plural in form but singular in meaning take a singular verb. Turn to page 752 in *Write Source*.

> **Circle** the subjects (nouns) that look plural but are singular in meaning. Then underline the singular verb that accompanies each one.

1   The (news) is good for people interested in math or science. Both are now

2   hot subjects. But mathematics (my particular favorite) has been around forever.

3   Math concepts first began when primitive peoples counted by 5's and 10's on

4   their hands. Later, Greek mathematicians, including Archimedes, Euclid, and

5   Pythagoras, made many advances in math. Their ideas crossed into astronomy,

6   physics, and other sciences.

7   Mathematics is the science of numbers. But mathematicians study more

8   than simple problems. Operations, relationships, and abstractions of numbers

9   are all factors in the big equation. Mathematics includes applied mathematics

10 and theoretical mathematics. Theoretical mathematicians study theories or do

11 research. Applied mathematicians apply math to practical uses. Economics is a

12 big field for applied mathematicians. Many mathematicians crunch numbers, or

13 analyze statistics, on Wall Street.

14 Physics owes its start to our Greek friend Archimedes, who invented

15 many mechanical devices such as levers and screws. Mechanics, one branch of

16 physics, covers only how objects move. Overall, physics deals with matter and

17 energy, and this science includes many branches—thermodynamics, nuclear

18 physics, geophysics, astrophysics, plasma physics, and cryogenics, among others.

19 Thermodynamics describes how heat and energy relate. Cryogenics is a cool

20 science that studies how objects react at temperatures below -238° F.

Subject-Verb Agreement 2

Compound subjects usually take a plural verb, and singular subjects take a singular verb. Turn to 752.1 in *Write Source*.

> **Circle** the correct singular or plural verb in the following sentences.

1. Past presidents, astronauts, and a United States air force general or two *(has,* *(have))* believed in unidentified flying objects (UFO's).

2. Gerald Ford and Jimmy Carter *(was, were)* trying to get the government to tell people more about UFO's.

3. But neither Ford nor Carter *(was, were)* president when he spoke about making government UFO facts available.

4. Ronald Reagan and Jimmy Carter *(claim, claims)* to have seen UFO's.

5. From 1952 to 1969, UFO reports and alien sightings *(was, were)* collected by the U.S. Air Force in Project Blue Book.

6. Now, government reports, including the Project Blue Book file, *(is, are)* available for study through the Freedom of Information Act.

7. In 1947 near Roswell, New Mexico, either a top-secret balloon or a UFO *(was, were)* recovered.

8. Supposedly, pieces of the "flying disk" and four or five alien bodies *(was, were)* taken to Wright-Patterson Air Force Base in Ohio.

9. Neither the UFO pieces nor a single alien body *(has, have)* been seen since.

10. Alien bodies and a spaceship *(is, are)* reported to still be at Area 51, a part of the highly secured air force base near Groom Lake, Nevada.

Extend: Write three to five sentences sharing your thoughts about UFO's and aliens. Use compound subjects (include at least one subject joined by *or* or *nor*). Check to be sure your subjects agree with their verbs.

Subject-Verb Agreement 3

Do not be confused by a word or words that come between a subject and a verb. Turn to 752.2 in *Write Source*.

> **Underline** the subject for each set of verbs in the sentences below and circle the verb that agrees with the subject. (Do not underline the conjunctions that join compound subjects.)

1. National <u>forests</u>, because of their size, (*offer,* *offers*) protection to many endangered species.

2. Rare and endangered species, from a tiny fern to a soaring eagle, (*find, finds*) a home in the Chequamegon-Nicolet National Forest in northern Wisconsin.

3. The goblin fern, a tiny plant that stands only one to two inches tall, (*live, lives*) in fewer than 50 places in the world.

4. The states in the western Great Lakes region (*has, have*) some of the best living conditions for the goblin fern.

5. Rare animals, including the timber wolf, (*live, lives*) in the Chequamegon forest.

6. The first timber wolf pack in Wisconsin since the 1960s, numbering about 15 wolves, (*was, were*) introduced in the 1980s.

7. The adventurous wolves of that first pack prospered and now (*number, numbers*) more than 200.

8. Wolf packs like to live in areas with few roads, and one such area deep within the forest hardwoods (*is, are*) near Bootjack Lake in the national forest.

9. The rivers and lakes of Chequamegon-Nicolet also (*offer, offers*) refuge to the bald eagle.

10. Some 689 nesting pairs of eagles, one of the largest concentrations in the United States, (*live, lives*) in Wisconsin.

Extend: Rewrite sentences 6 and 7 so that the singular subject is plural and the plural subject is singular.

Review: Subject-Verb Agreement

> **Underline** the subject for each set of verbs in parentheses; then circle the correct verb (singular or plural). (Do not underline the conjunctions that join compound subjects.)

1   Malorie and Emma *(are, is)* best friends. Each *(have, has)* known the

2   other since they attended nursery school together. Now that both of them *(are,*

3   *is)* older, they know that any friendship like theirs *(are, is)* dependent upon

4   trust and reliability. As trust and reliability grow, the friendship *(become,*

5   *becomes)* stronger. All of their friends *(wonder, wonders)* how two people who

6   are so different could remain friends for so long. Malorie says each of them

7   *(complements, complement)* the other. Emma thinks they share important basic

8   beliefs; they may look and act completely different, but their values *(is, are)* the

9   same. She also believes their friendship is not that unusual. Several of their

10   friends also *(share, shares)* long-term friendships. "Everyone," says Emma, "*(is,*

11   *are)* capable of having a long-term friendship; you just have to be yourself."

12   Neither Malorie nor Emma *(take, takes)* their friendship for granted. Friends are

13   good, and good friends *(is, are)* even better.

> **Underline** the subject in each sentence below; then circle the verb that agrees with the delayed subject.

1. In the library *(were, was)* 10 biology students preparing for an exam.

2. *(Is, Are)* either of the boys attending the basketball game tonight?

3. In our class *(is, are)* three students who will be studying in Spain.

4. *(Has, Have)* your mother or father given you permission to take driver's

education this summer?

Pretest: Pronoun-Antecedent Agreement

> **Underline** the correct pronoun (or pronoun and verb) in each pair below. Then circle the antecedent that the pronoun refers to.

1. The two boys are sloppy; (neither) cleans (<u>his</u>, *their*) room.

2. The Martin twins are outdoorsmen; both spend most of (*his*, *their*) time in the woods.

3. Good gas mileage and reliability—(*that's*, *these are*) the hallmarks of a good car.

4. I'll take one of those blue shirts if (*they are*, *it is*) available.

5. Snakes' forked tongues have a dual purpose: (*they are*, *it is*) used to smell as well as to taste food.

6. Either Cindy or Nancy knows (*her*, *their*) way around the dance floor.

7. One of the walls looks shabby; (*it needs*, *they need*) repair.

8. Neither Susan nor Sheryl complains when (*she is*, *they are*) hungry.

9. Both planes had (*their*, *its*) interiors redecorated.

10. Each of the planes had (*their*, *its*) interior redecorated.

11. Mary and her sister took (*their*, *her*) brother to the concert.

12. When you find one of the sweaters I loaned you, please return (*them*, *it*) to me.

13. A person needs (*their*, *his or her*) privacy.

14. When Cory and Catherine got married, we all attended (*her*, *their*) wedding.

15. Each salesperson presented (*their*, *his or her*) new products.

16. Bring me one of those apples; make sure (*it is*, *they are*) fresh.

17. Neither of his cars (*were*, *was*) in very good condition.

Pronoun-Antecedent Agreement 1

Each pronoun has an antecedent that the pronoun refers to or replaces. Turn to page 756 in *Write Source* for more information and examples.

> **Underline** the correct answer in each of the following sentences. Write the antecedent above the pronoun you underline.

1. For the job hunter to get the best possible job, *(he or she needs, they need)* to
   (job) hunter
   have three or four job offers from which to choose.

2. Everyone owes it to *(himself or herself, themselves)* to become acquainted with
   all phases of the job-hunting process.

3. Both Ashley and her friend Shelli use newspaper ads to find new job leads,
   which *(she pursues, they pursue)* with a phone call and a letter.

4. The Internet now has many help-wanted sites, so *(they serve, it serves)* job
   hunters, too.

5. Job hunters make *(his or her, their)* availability known by placing information
   about themselves and *(his or her, their)* skills in newspapers or on Internet sites.

6. Most colleges have good placement services because *(they understand,*
   it understands) that finding a good job is the major reason *(their, its)* students
   come to college.

7. Some colleges offer *(its, their)* students a complete job-placement service,
   extending for years after students have graduated.

8. Other college offices, however, think *(its, their)* responsibility is completed when
   they place a student once after *(he or she has, they have)* graduated.

9. A private employment agency charges *(its, their)* customers only when *(he or she*
   gets, they get) jobs.

10. Although many people are unaware of this fact, the U.S. government offers all
    (its, their) citizens a free employment service.

Pronoun-Antecedent Agreement 2

Each personal pronoun has an antecedent that the pronoun clearly refers to or replaces. Turn to page 756 in *Write Source* for more information and examples.

> **Underline** the correct personal pronouns below and write the antecedent above each.

1. *ants*
   Ants are incredibly diverse insects; (it, <u>they</u>) consist of 20,000 different species

   and are located throughout the world.

2. Most ant species make *(its, their)* nests underground.

3. Most species have a queen; *(she, it)* lives the longest, from about 10 to 20 years.

4. Worker ants from different communities often fight one another when *(each, they)*

   meet.

5. A fierce battle can ensue, and *(it, they)* may take many lives.

6. Army ants are such fierce fighters that other insects have come to fear *(it, them)*.

7. Some army ants live in clusters above ground; *(it, their)* queen and *(its, her)*

   brood lie amid the large cluster of bodies.

8. A harvester ant feeds on the seeds *(they collect, it collects)*.

9. Some ants collect larvae from other ant colonies; *(it brings, they bring)* *(it, them)*

   home and use them as slaves when they are full grown.

10. One species of the Amazon ant becomes so reliant on its slave ants that *(they, it)*

    can care for neither itself nor *(their, its)* young.

Extend: Write three or four sentences about ants (or some other insect). Underline each personal pronoun and write its antecedent above it.

Pronoun References

A writer must be careful not to confuse the reader with references that are unclear or ambiguous. (*Ambiguous* means having more than one meaning.) Ambiguous pronoun reference results when it is not clear which word is being referred to by the pronoun in the sentence. Turn to page 195 in *Write Source*.

> **As he drove his car up to the service window, it made a rattling sound.**
> (It isn't clear what "made a rattling sound," the car or the window.)

> **As he drove up to the service window, his car made a rattling sound.**
> (Now the reader knows the car made the rattling sound.)

Rewrite each of the sentences below so that it is clear which word the pronoun refers to. (You will have to replace the ambiguous pronoun with the appropriate noun in several sentences.)

1. The team moved the wrestling mat off the gym floor so that it could be cleaned.

The team moved the wrestling mat off the gym floor so that the floor could be cleaned. (or) so that the mat could be cleaned.

2. Tara entered her program into the computer, and it went completely haywire.

3. Alina asked her mother if she could carry one of the boxes for her.

4. All calendars list the holidays if they are worthwhile.

5. Check all your papers for obvious writing errors so that your teacher can enjoy reading them.

Review: Pronoun-Antecedent Agreement

> **Underline** the correct pronoun (and verb if appropriate) in each pair below. Then circle the antecedent that the pronoun refers to.

1. When (Gary and Kurt) returned to (his, _their_) table, some of the pizza was missing.

2. Either of the boys could have found (his, their) bat and ball if (he, they) had really tried.

3. Anybody can attend the seminar as long as (they have, she or he has) permission.

4. Some people use scarecrows to protect (its, their) gardens.

5. Rafael read the magazine from beginning to end before lending (him, it) to Syd.

6. Everyone should find (his or her, their) assigned seat.

7. Because a weeping willow can be so messy, (they are, it is) often shunned by homeowners.

8. Charlene was using (her, our) old toothbrush to clean the heating vents.

9. Some automobile dealers offer (its, their) customers free car-care workshops.

10. Bobbi decided she didn't want one of the items after all, so she returned (it, them) to the mall.

11. He said the sewing machines will be good as new as soon as (he is, they are) repaired.

12. Neither Robert nor his brothers ever managed to take care of (his, their) dog.

Pretest: Sentence Combining

Combine each of the following groups of sentences. Use the sentence-combining technique indicated in parentheses.

1. Fire is hot. Fire is wild. Fire is violent. *(Use a series.)*

Fire is hot, wild, and violent.

2. You can often put out a home fire with the right kind of fire extinguisher. This works if the fire is small when it is detected. *(Use an introductory phrase or clause.)*

_____

_____

3. We keep several fire extinguishers around the house to put out small fires. We keep them to provide peace of mind. *(Use correlative conjunctions.)*

_____

_____

4. Electrical fires and those involving flammable liquids should be put out with the spray from a carbon-dioxide or a dry chemical extinguisher. These fires cannot be extinguished with water. *(Use a relative pronoun.)*

_____

_____

5. A carbon-dioxide extinguisher releases a blanket of carbon dioxide. This type of fire extinguisher keeps air from reaching the fire. *(Use a participial phrase.)*

_____

_____

6. Fire can be a terrifying enemy. Fire is normally one of our greatest allies. *(Use an appositive.)*

_____

_____

Sentence Combining 1

Sentence combining, which can be done in a variety of ways, is one of the most effective writing techniques you can practice. Turn to page 83 in *Write Source*.

> **Combine** the following sentences using the methods indicated.

1. *(Use a semicolon and a conjunctive adverb.)* The most popular pets are dogs, cats, parakeets, and fish. Unusual pets like snakes, alligators, and monkeys are becoming more popular.

_____

_____

_____

_____

2. *(Use the correlative conjunctions "not only," "but also.")* Pets can improve a person's morale. They can also lower a person's blood pressure.

_____

_____

3. *(Repeat a key word.)* Pets are great therapy for seniors. They are especially valuable for seniors who are in care centers.

_____

_____

4. *(Use a series.)* Pets guard property. They assist blind people. They keep rodents away.

_____

_____

5. *(Use a relative pronoun.)* Children in Japan tame mice for pets. They often teach them to dance.

_____

_____

Extend: Write four brief sentences about pets. Use two different methods to combine them into two sentences.

Sentence Combining 2

Using a variety of sentence-combining methods can create sentences that work together to build a clear, interesting paragraph that reads smoothly. Turn to page 83 in *Write Source*.

> **Read** the following paragraphs. Combine sentences to create a paragraph that reads smoothly. (Not all sentences need combining; slight rewording is acceptable.)

1. It was before the 1800s. Fires could destroy whole settlements. A fire would break out. All the people in the community would hurry to the scene. They arranged themselves in a line. The line started at a source of water. The line ended at the fire. The people passed buckets of water to each other to put the fire out.

_____

_____

_____

_____

_____

_____

2. Now fire departments respond to fires and other emergencies. The fire departments consist of well-trained professional firefighters and well-designed equipment. People may be trapped in cars after an accident. Firefighters rescue them. Firefighters also aid victims of tornadoes and hurricanes. They help victims of floods and earthquakes, too.

_____

_____

_____

_____

_____

_____

Review: Sentence Combining

Fire departments work hard to prevent fires.
They enforce safety laws.
Professional firefighters teach people about fire dangers.
They hope this work will help prevent fire losses.
Every year, fires kill hundreds of people.
Fires injure thousands of people, too.
Fires also destroy millions of dollars' worth of property.

1. Use a series to combine three or more similar ideas.

Every year, fires kill hundreds of people, injure thousands more,

and destroy millions of dollars' worth of property.

2. Use a relative pronoun to introduce a subordinate idea.

_____

_____

3. Use an introductory phrase or clause for a less important idea.

_____

_____

4. Use a semicolon. (Also use a conjunctive adverb if appropriate.)

_____

_____

5. Use correlative conjunctions to compare or contrast two ideas.

_____

_____

6. Use an appositive phrase to emphasize an idea.

_____

_____

Pretest: Sentence Problems

> **Identify** the problems in the following sentences. Use *F* for fragment, *CS* for comma splice, *RO* for run-on sentence, *RS* for rambling sentence, *W* for wordiness, and *MM* for misplaced modifier.

    _F_   **1.** When the calendar changed at the end of the year 999.

    _____   **2.** Most people didn't know what year it was, and in Europe there were only a few educated people who knew the date, and they were concerned that going from three digits to four might destroy the symmetry of the universe, and they also worried about having enough space on documents to write four digits instead of three.

    _____   **3.** Arabic numbers were being used for the first time the concept of "0" was baffling to many they wondered how a zero could stand for nothing.

    _____   **4.** Things were not too civilized in Europe during that time and that period in Europe was called the Dark Ages because it was an uncivilized, lawless, barbaric time when laws were broken regularly and people cared little for others.

    _____   **5.** Common people survived and never bathed with only the clothes on their backs.

    _____   **6.** Sanitation was nonexistent, as was clean water, the average peasant spent most of each day trying to get enough to eat.

    _____   **7.** Families slept together in one room along with the family's livestock and strangers who came in for shelter using lice-infested straw pallets for beds.

    _____   **8.** *Beowulf,* an epic poem, written in Old English about 1,200 years ago.

    _____   **9.** The Chinese people from Asia invented some kind of gunpowder about 1,000 years ago, which they used for fireworks and colorful blasts in the night sky instead of using it to power guns and other weapons.

    _____   **10.** Huge fireworks displays marked the dawn of the year 2000 there probably was no such fanfare when the previous millennium began in 1000.

> **Correct** each of the problem sentences above by rewriting it in a better way on the lines below and on the next page.

1. _When the calendar changed at the end of the year 999, most people didn't know what year it was._

2. _____
   _____
   _____
   _____
   _____
   _____

3. _____
   _____
   _____

4. _____
   _____

5. _____
   _____

6. _____
   _____

7. _____
   _____
   _____

8. _____
   _____

9. _____
   _____

10. _____
    _____

Run-On Sentences

Run-on sentences are actually two or more sentences joined without proper punctuation—or a connecting word. Turn to page 87 in *Write Source*.

> **Correct** each run-on sentence. Insert a semicolon, add a comma with a coordinating conjunction, or create two sentences.

1. The Bermuda Triangle is a part of the Atlantic Ocean. It lies off the southern tip of Florida between Bermuda and Puerto Rico.

2. Many strange things have happened on and over this stretch of water many disappearances have been documented over the years.

3. Descriptions of glowing clouds, equipment failures, and extremely choppy seas are common elements of many Bermuda Triangle incidents many pilots also report losing sight of land even when flying along the coast.

4. In 1944, the Cuban ship *Rubicon* was found drifting in the Triangle without a trace of its crew only a dog remained on board.

5. On December 5, 1945, five Navy planes carrying 14 crew members disappeared they broadcast a confused message and were never heard from again.

6. Even Christopher Columbus figures into the puzzle his ship's log includes observations of fire in the sky and glowing white water while sailing through the Triangle.

7. Apollo astronauts in space reported unusual wave activity in the Bermuda Triangle they had no explanation for it.

8. The Triangle is still active scientists and enthusiasts continue to study the phenomenon.

9. How do planes disappear without wreckage how do crews vanish without a trace?

10. Perhaps one day we'll know the answer until then, it remains a mystery.

Comma Splices

A *comma splice* results when two independent clauses are connected ("spliced") with only a comma when a comma is not enough. A period, a semicolon, a comma with a coordinating conjunction (*and, but, or . . .*), or a semicolon and a conjunctive adverb (*however, moreover, besides . . .*) must be used to fix a comma splice. The more closely related the sentences are to one another, the more appropriate it is to use a semicolon. Turn to page 87 in *Write Source*.

> **Identify** and correct any comma splices by adding conjunctions or appropriate punctuation where necessary in the following paragraphs.

1 Jackie Robinson grew up in Pasadena, California. He was the first

2 African American to play major league baseball. His mother and four older

3 siblings worked hard to make a living, Jackie pitched in to help, selling

4 newspapers on the street corner. Jackie joined a neighborhood gang called

5 the Pepper Street Gang, taking and reselling golf balls from golf courses

6 and throwing fruit at cars got them in trouble with the police. Eventually

7 a teacher inspired him to leave the gang, telling him a strong individual

8 didn't belong in a gang.

9 Jackie lettered in football, baseball, basketball, and track in high

10 school, he impressed a lot of scouts while playing football in junior college,

11 landing him a football scholarship at UCLA. Jackie became UCLA's first

12 athlete to letter in four sports, many people were shocked and disappointed

13 when he left college early to take a job at a government youth camp in

14 order to help his mother financially.

15 Worried about being called tough on the football field but cowardly on

16 the battlefield, he refused to use an injured ankle as a military exemption

17 and was drafted. Jackie failed to qualify for Officers Candidate School, he

18 and heavyweight champ Joe Louis called for an investigation, the inquiry

19 uncovered illegal practices, and Jackie spent several years as an officer.

Sentence Fragments

A fragment is a group of words incorrectly used as a sentence. Because it lacks a subject, a verb, or another key element, the thought is incomplete. Turn to page 86 in *Write Source*.

Underline the fragments in the following paragraph. On the lines below, rewrite the paragraph, making the fragments into complete sentences. Add a subject or a verb or connect the fragment to a related sentence in the paragraph.

Hundreds of people have reported seeing a large animal in Loch Ness. A lake in northern Scotland. The Loch Ness monster, nicknamed "Nessie." Observers say the creature has a long, slender neck. Like a dinosaur. It also has one or two humps and flippers. Scientific expeditions have used sonar to explore the lake. Have detected large moving objects. Not sure whether the objects are one large creature or a school of fish. Underwater photographs have been taken, although many experts question their validity. Despite the doubts about Nessie's very existence. Tourists still flock to Loch Ness in the hopes of catching a glimpse.

_____

_____

_____

_____

_____

_____

_____

_____

_____

_____

_____

Acceptable Sentence Fragments

Is it ever acceptable to use fragments? Yes, when you have good reason. Single words or phrases set off as sentences can have a dramatic effect. You can also use fragments when you write dialogue, because people often use incomplete thoughts when they talk. Turn to page 86 in *Write Source*.

> **Read** the following passages in which the writer deliberately uses fragments (shown in italics). Tell why you think the author uses each fragment.

1. "Everyone in that family, including my three cousins, could draw a horse. *Beautifully.*"

—Annie Dillard

_____

_____

_____

2. Mrs. Stokes: Weezie, come get your lunch, girl.
Weezie: *No time. Lots of homework.*

_____

_____

_____

3. *A place to rest in the middle of the lagoon. Drips from the oars.* An egret flaps its wings where it stands.

_____

_____

_____

4. *"Hurry! In the bedroom!"* Murray pleaded as he ushered the ambulance attendants in.

_____

_____

_____

Extend: Write a short passage in which you deliberately use a few fragments for special effect. With a classmate, discuss how well they work.

Rambling Sentences

Rambling sentences keep going and going, which results in a muddled, monotonous message. To correct rambling sentences, remove some of the *and*'s, fix the punctuation, and reword parts when necessary. Turn to page 87 in *Write Source*.

> **Rewrite** and clarify the rambling sentences below.

1. I returned my overdue books to the library and I paid my fine and I looked around for a while and then checked out three new books.

I returned my overdue books to the library and paid my fine. After looking

around for a while, I checked out three new books.

2. Most of the teachers and administrators attended the ceremony and so did other school personnel including the aides and custodians and even the cooks.

_____

_____

3. Eligia was stopped in traffic and just sat there for an hour and he listened to CD's and hoped his boss would understand the problem he was facing.

_____

_____

4. Karl didn't hear his alarm and woke up late and rushed like crazy but still missed his first class.

_____

_____

5. It was raining hard and the wind was strong and my umbrella ripped and I got totally soaked.

_____

_____

6. Night fell quickly and we could see the campfires dotting the hillside and hear the drums pounding in the distance and we rose to dance.

_____

_____

Review: Sentence Problems 1

Edit the following paragraphs. Correct sentence fragments, comma splices, run-ons, and rambling sentences. Add or delete punctuation, capitalization, and words.

1   As a small child, he had only eaten toast for breakfast. Now, however, with

2   a need for more energy. ̶H̶e has begun eating granola, fruit, and orange juice.

3   Along with his new eating habits, his looks are also beginning to change he

4   wears his hair a bit longer in back and thinner on top and his shoes are those

5   funny-looking sandals. That are good for your posture. He thinks about this.

6   As he sits gazing out at the backyard, which the neighbor kid with the blue-

7   streaked hair mows every Saturday for a "sawbuck." He wonders if the kid

8   knows that "sawbuck" is a slang term for a ten-dollar bill.

9   Maybe his younger brother Kevin is right in his appraisal and maybe he

10   is old-fashioned and way, way out of step. He and Kevin had gone out with

11   their parents the night before, Kevin had walked into the restaurant and had

12   scanned his brother's clothes and posture, in addition, he had even seemed to

13   scan his brother's thoughts, with slow-mounting amusement, Kevin had said,

14   "You look so . . . granola." Trying to disguise his obvious embarrassment, the

15   older brother grabbed his keys and headed for his truck in the parking lot. He

16   would be glad when Kevin aged more and understood more but Kevin was the

17   kind of guy who exercised, he had been the kind of kid who played every sport

18   in high school, and he probably still played a lot of sports and, of course, Kevin

19   had always eaten a good breakfast.

Misplaced Modifiers

You know what happens when you drag your feet along the bottom of a lake. Things become murky and obscure. That's what happens in your reader's brain when you accidentally misplace modifiers. To ensure clarity, you must be able to recognize misplaced modifiers so they can be moved or reworded accordingly. Turn to page 88 in *Write Source*.

> **Locate** and underline the misplaced modifier in each of the following sentences. Then revise each sentence by moving the misplaced modifier to its proper location. (Make other changes to the sentence as needed.)

1. The books for the new students <u>with course-identification numbers</u> are piled in stacks.

   The books for the new students are piled in stacks with course-identification numbers.

2. Athletes must train hard to make the Olympic team for many years.

   _____

   _____

3. Quentin planted roses in his backyard garden named for Queen Elizabeth.

   _____

   _____

4. We will be visiting several four-year colleges that I am considering attending over the summer.

   _____

   _____

5. My father has gone to the library every Sunday to check out a book for years.

   _____

   _____

Extend: Experiment with misplaced modifiers in three sentences you write about school. Exchange papers with a classmate and correct one another's misplaced modifiers.

Dangling Modifiers

Dangling modifiers appear to modify the wrong word. Turn to page 88 in *Write Source*.

> **Locate** and underline the dangling modifier in each of the following sentences. Revise each sentence so that the modifier clearly modifies the word it was intended to. Add or change words as necessary.

1. After swimming in the lake nearly all afternoon, Bill's mother called him.

After swimming in the lake nearly all afternoon, Bill heard his mother call him.

2. While listening to my newest CD, someone came to the door.

3. Having never flown before, the flight attendant was especially nice to me.

4. Though only 10 years old, my mother taught me to quilt.

5. After running three laps around the track, the coach signaled us to head for the showers.

6. Failing to see the stop sign, the car rammed into the side of an oncoming truck.

Wordiness & Deadwood

Wordiness and deadwood fill up lots of space but do not add anything new or important to the overall meaning of a sentence.

> **Place** brackets around the unnecessary words in the paragraphs below.

1   My mother, a native New Yorker, [who has lived in New York her

2   whole life,] recently went to Africa on an African safari. Many people

3   thought this was an odd trip for an elderly woman. I don't know when or

4   how the idea was first introduced to her, but as soon as she heard about

5   the safari trip, she began reading everything she could get her hands on

6   about Africa. The safari, which was organized last year, was composed of

7   15 senior citizens, none of whom had ever heard of a zebu (a breed of

8   ox), and most of whom thought the Watusi (an African tribe) was just a

9   1960s dance.

10   My mother and her fellow senior citizen explorers were very impressed

11   with the wealth of natural beauty and living animal life on the African

12   plains and in the jungles. They were also impressed with Africa's animal

13   parks and game reserves that protect and help animals to survive from

14   human hunters who are a real threat to their existence. Herd animals

15   such as zebras, wildebeest, and antelope are also protected from hunters

16   within the borders of game reserves.

17   My mother got back from her African journey and returned with

18   wonderful memories of a unique culture and wilderness that she will

19   remember for a long time.

Extend: Select something you have recently written. Exchange it for a classmate's paper and place brackets around any obvious wordiness or deadwood in your partner's work.

Unparallel Construction 1

Parallelism is the repeating of similar words, phrases, or clauses to add balance and emphasis to your writing. Inconsistent or unparallel construction occurs when the words, phrases, or clauses being used change in the middle of a sentence. Turn to pages 85 and 601 in *Write Source*.

> **We wanted to sing, to dance, and to tell stories around the campfire.** (repetition of infinitives)

> **Janice looked under the table, in the pantry, and behind the sofa.** (repetition of prepositional phrases)

> **Winning the contest, receiving the trophy, and making a thank-you speech were exciting events for Megan.** (repetition of gerund phrases)

Underline the parallel structures in the following sentences. Explain what word groups are repeated in each sentence.

1. Some students wanted <u>to decorate for the banquet</u>, <u>to serve appetizers</u>, and <u>to hire a comedian</u>.

Infinitive phrases are repeated. (or) Phrases beginning with "to" are

repeated.

2. Washing the dishes, feeding the cat, and taking out the garbage are my chores.

3. Great-tasting turnips and odd-looking parsnips grow well in our garden.

4. I have a grandma who listens well, who is wise, and who crochets scarves.

5. Having a bicycle to ride on campus is more useful than having a car to drive.

6. Our mother had explained, pleaded, and commanded.

7. The woods are filled with towering oaks, singing birds, and winding trails.

Unparallel Construction 2

Inconsistent or unparallel construction occurs when the kinds of words, phrases, or clauses being used change in the middle of a sentence. Turn to pages 85 and 601 in *Write Source*.

Complete the following sentences so that all the parts are parallel.

1. The police officer at the corner of 42nd Avenue and 6th Street directs traffic, chats with pedestrians, and ___*helps seniors cross the street.*___

2. Waiting for the bus, standing in the rain, and _____ are not my favorite activities.

3. We strolled through Central Park to Strawberry Fields, stopped at a sidewalk cafe for coffee, and _____

_____

4. Reading the book was enjoyable; _____ the paper about it was difficult.

5. We must measure the room, order the rug, and _____

6. Listen to me when I tell you to look forward to the future, when I tell you to plan to work hard, and _____

7. Yes, of course, there are times when I am lonely, and there are times when I am bothered by the quiet, but there are also times _____

_____

8. Turn the stove down to low, let the applesauce simmer, and _____

_____

9. Tired and sore, the bicyclist sat under a tree; _____ , the other biker drank from her water bottle.

10. I love the smell of grass after it's mowed; I love the sound _____ ; and I love the sight _____

Unparallel Construction 3

There's a good chance your writing will improve if you use repetition of similar words, phrases, and clauses. Parallel construction adds rhythm, emphasis, unity, and impact to your writing. Professional writers use this kind of repetition to give their passages impact. Public speakers use it to give their messages rhythm and emphasis. Turn to pages 85 and 601 in *Write Source*.

> **Study** the parts of each sentence below. Imitate the models as well as you can.

1. Goldilocks sat in Papa Bear's chair, but it was too hard. She sat in Mama Bear's chair, but it was too soft. She sat in Baby Bear's chair, and it was just right.

—as retold by mothers and fathers everywhere

_____

_____

_____

2. "If you can laugh at it, you can live with it."   —Erma Bombeck

_____

_____

3. "The test of our progress is not whether we add more to the abundance of those who have much; it is whether we provide enough for those who have too little."

—Franklin D. Roosevelt

_____

_____

4. "Once there was a lot of sound in my mother's house, a lot of coming and going, feasting and talking."   —N. Scott Momaday, "My Kiowa Grandmother"

_____

_____

_____

Extend: If you like parallel structures, look for examples as you read. Record the best examples in a notebook for future reference.

Review: Sentence Problems 2

> **Rewrite** the following sentences to eliminate misplaced or dangling modifiers.

1. Working hard to pass the exam, John's mother agreed to help him.

Working hard to pass the exam, John persuaded his mother to help him.

2. The woodpecker is causing damage to our wooden boat we keep trying to get rid of.

3. Hernando tripped over his skateboard running down the street.

4. Before leaving Montana for vacation, the horses needed grooming.

> **Put** brackets around any words that are unnecessary in the following sentences. When necessary, rewrite sentence parts adding your changes above the line.

1. Regardless of any opposing opinions, I am going to do what I think is right, and I don't care what anyone else thinks.

2. With winter fast approaching, it's a good idea to prepare our cars for the cold months ahead.

3. Due to the fact that the storm knocked out our electricity and the electrical power to our area, it seems that we should be in the process of trying to find some dry ice for the purpose of keeping our milk and other perishables that might spoil chilled.

Make all the words parallel to the first word in each set. Then use your words in a sentence.

      jumping throwing

1. running, ~~jumped~~, ~~throw~~   *Running, jumping, and throwing are skills many*

    athletes need.

2. rakes, listening, took _____

_____

3. played cards, watching a video, eat dinner _____

_____

Create sentences that are parallel in structure. Follow the directions for each sentence.

1. Use infinitive phrases: _____

_____

_____

2. Use participial phrases: _____

_____

_____

3. Use prepositional phrases: _____

_____

_____

4. Use gerund phrases: _____

_____

_____

Pretest: Shifts in Construction

Shifts in construction can be shifts in *number* (singular to plural, plural to singular), in *person* (using a combination of 1st, 2nd, and 3rd persons), in *tense* (using an inappropriate combination of tenses), or in *voice* (active to passive, passive to active).

> **Correct** the first underlined part in each sentence below by writing the correction above it. (The two underlined parts in each sentence represent an incorrect shift in construction.) On the blank, identify the kind of shift: number, person, tense, or voice.

number 1. When a student works hard in a class, it is a shame if they have
   students work
   trouble taking exams.

_____ 2. One must not bring a cart loaded with groceries to the express lane, or you might be asked to go to another checkout.

_____ 3. While the librarian waits for her computer to download the information, she cataloged the new reference books.

_____ 4. The fans were shouting and waved their hands at the camera during the seventh-inning stretch.

_____ 5. We would shop at the mall with the designer outlets if they were not so far from our home.

_____ 6. If you are told by your teacher to finish your paper by Friday, but you forget it, he or she can lower your grade.

_____ 7. A person may not truly learn a lesson until something very painful happens to them.

_____ 8. We skated on the frozen pond; then we were drinking hot chocolate in the lodge.

_____ 9. The seeds were eaten by the birds, and they build nests nearby.

_____ 10. We wanted to sing, but she didn't know the words to the songs.

Shifts in Verb Tense 1

Consistent verb tenses clearly establish time in your writing. When verb tenses change without warning or for no reason, readers can become confused. Turn to 718.4 in *Write Source* for more information about past, present, and future verb tenses.

> **Underline** the verb in the first sentence of each pair. Change the verb tense in the second sentence to be consistent with the first. Finally, identify the tense that is used.

present **1.** The Channel Tunnel is a railway tunnel beneath the English
Channel. The tunnel ~~linked~~ *links* England and France.

_____ **2.** The "Chunnel" opened in 1994. How many passengers will ride the tunnel trains that year?

_____ **3.** The tunnel has three types of trains. One kind, the shuttle train, carried automobiles, trucks, buses, and their passengers.

_____ **4.** The other two types of trains were designed for high-speed passenger traffic. The trip through the tunnel takes about one-half hour.

_____ **5.** To take the train, you will enter the tunnel in Folkestone, England. On the French side, you go into the tunnel at Coquelles, near Calais.

_____ **6.** The tunnel measures nearly 31 miles from entrance to entrance. Nearly 24 of those miles lay underwater.

_____ **7.** The structure consists of three parallel tubes. Two tubes will accommodate the railroads.

_____ **8.** A third tube lies between the other two. It supplied fresh air and maintenance access to the rail tubes.

_____ **9.** The third tube will provide for emergency evacuation. The design of this structure contributes to the safety of the riders.

_____ **10.** The three tubes generally lie about 130 feet beneath the seabed. Rings of concrete or iron formed a continuous lining in the tubes.

Shifts in Verb Tense 2

Tense shifts, also called tense sequences, are sometimes necessary to help a writer show more than one time in a sentence. Just make sure your tense shifts are correct. Turn to 718.4 in *Write Source*.

 He was certain that he had left me a message.
(The first verb *was* shows past action. The second verb *had left* shows an action that occurred before the past action. This verb sequence past/past perfect is often used.)

Place a verb in the blank space in each sentence below. Choose a verb tense that differs from the first verb in the sentence and makes clear that the two actions described in the sentence occur at different times.

1. Although the dynamite had exploded, the building _____*remained*_____ intact.

2. The snow is accumulating, so the plows _____ out.

3. It rained here yesterday, but the sun _____ most of the time.

4. We lost this week's game, but we _____ when we play next week.

5. Because it rained all week long, the playing field _____ into a quagmire.

6. John failed his driver's test last week, but he _____ to take it again next week.

7. Since Yolanda had sprained her ankle two days before, she _____ yesterday's track meet.

8. If Terrell wins the election, it _____ the third time in a row he has been elected.

9. Based on the winning margin in the past two elections, I think he _____ this time as well.

10. Because a thunderstorm had darkened the sky, the maintenance crew _____ the stadium lights on early.

Shifts in Verb Tense 3

Tense shifts made for no reason can add confusion to your writing. Changes in tense to describe time changes in your writing are, however, necessary. For more on tenses, turn to 718.4 in *Write Source*.

> **We *will finish* our homework before we *go* to the movie.**
> (The verb tense shifts from future to present.)

> **My mom *had declined* the invitation before I even *read* it.**
> (The verb tense shifts from past perfect to past.)

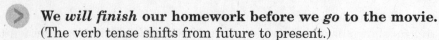

Underline and label the two verb tenses used in the following sentences.

        future perfect   *present*

1. The train <u>will be</u> delayed because the railbed <u>is</u> under water.

2. I hope Dad will buy a new car soon.

3. Mom is certain she added the eggs to the cake.

4. Grandma <u>remembers</u> that she <u>came</u> to the United States in 1949.

5. Will you please fix the faucet before you go to work?

6. Claire claimed she had written all her thank-you letters.

7. Mr. Dickens has remembered that his mother will have a birthday tomorrow.

8. The state of Alaska has offered invitations to all distance runners; Alaska wants these athletes to run in the Solstice Marathon.

9. After the gate had been opened, the horses ran out.

10. We will wear earplugs when we mow the lawn next time.

11. Before the exam begins, we will want to go over our notes again.

12. The stew tasted strong because so many root vegetables had been added.

13. The stapler is out of staples, so someone will have to fill it.

14. If she hangs the sheets on the line, they will smell like fresh air and sunshine.

15. He said, "Give me a break."

16. If he takes that long to pack again, the train will have left without him.

Pronoun Shifts 1

In a well-written sentence, pronouns should not shift in number, person, or gender. Turn to pages 708 and 710 in *Write Source*.

> **Replace** the underlined pronouns with ones that match the number, person, and gender of the other pronoun in the following sentences. (The first five antecedents are in italics.) Also change any verbs as necessary. If an underlined pronoun is correct, write **C** above it.

1. *You* may be able to tune a guitar, but can <u>one</u> *you* tune a piano?

2. When *a person* plays guitar for a while, <u>they</u> should know how to tune a guitar.

3. *Anybody* can tune <u>their</u> guitar in a few simple steps.

4. An in-tune guitar means that all strings are at *their* proper tension so that <u>they</u> produce the correct pitches, or sounds.

5. Every *guitarist* starts the tuning process with the sixth string (the thickest one) on <u>your</u> guitar.

6. And because you are probably an ace guitarist in a rockin' band, <u>one</u> should do an absolute, or concert, tuning.

7. When concert tuning, one uses a tuning fork (A or E) to determine the correct tone for that string, no matter what guitar <u>they</u> play.

8. When tuning her guitar, Julie strikes the E fork on <u>his</u> knee and places the tuning fork's base on the guitar near the strings.

9. Julie then plays the guitar string that matches the fork's pitch, and <u>you</u> try to match the tone by tightening or loosening the string.

10. Peter brings in his guitar. He sits next to Julie, and both match the tone of the fifth string. Then <u>they</u> tune the other strings, one after the other.

Pronoun Shifts 2

Using indefinite pronouns is tricky because they can easily shift in number or person as you write. Turn to pages 754 and 756 in *Write Source*. See 754.2 for information on which indefinite pronouns are singular, plural, or either singular or plural.

> **Circle** the correct pronoun in each sentence below.

---

1. Before anybody buys a used car, (*he or she,* *they*) should inspect it thoroughly.

2. You might begin by looking for rust on the car. If someone painted the car recently, it could mean that (*he or she, they*) may have been covering up damage.

3. Someone should close the car's doors, open its windows, and pop its trunk. If one sees something not fitting properly, (*he or she, they*) may need to ask more questions about the car's history.

4. For example, if one of the car's doors fits badly, it may indicate that (*it was, they were*) damaged.

5. Everyone should check tailpipes for black, gooey soot, and (*they, he or she*) should also check the car's oil level.

6. However, be careful not to wear (*your, his or her, their*) light-colored clothes when doing this kind of check.

7. When checking headlights, taillights, brake lights, backup lights, and directional signals, several friends might work together so that (*he or she, they*) can complete the checks quickly and accurately.

8. Just remember, none of the tasks mentioned above are really that aggravating if (*it helps, they help*) you avoid a buyer's biggest nightmare—buying a lemon.

Extend: Write three to five sentences on how you would go about inspecting an item that you are interested in buying. Think about how you would use the item. Add your own special inspection points. Check for pronoun shifts in your writing.

Pronoun Shifts 3

Within a sentence, a pronoun must agree in number, person, and gender with the word it refers to—its antecedent. Turn to 756.1 and 756.2 in *Write Source*. Also see 754.1 for information on collective nouns and how to determine if they are singular or plural.

> **Circle** the correct pronoun in each sentence below.

1. The team was awarded a trophy for (*its,* *their*) winning record.

2. The coach awarded each player (*his or her, their*) letter.

3. Both the players and coach expressed (*their, his*) pride in the team.

4. All team members had something good to say about (*its, their*) coach.

5. The team promised to do (*its, their*) best the following season.

6. The coach gave the team the privilege of keeping (*its, their*) uniform jerseys.

7. Both Nassir and Joel rode down the freeway in silence until (*he, they*) reached the O-Kee-Doke Diner.

8. Neither Nassir nor the other patrons knew that (*he was, they were*) in for a big surprise.

9. Along with the entree, all the diners could have (*your, their*) choice of garlic mashed potatoes or roasted peppers.

10. Uncle Raymond drove (*her, his*) truck on the gravel road while the kids and Auntie Fay screamed (*her, their*) usual—"Whoopie!"

11. A ballet dancer is one of those athletes who must stay in excellent condition and keep on (*their, his or her*) toes.

12. Tonight either the Blue Soxs or the Mustangs will receive (*its, your*) official notification to move to Miller.

13. John lost his keys because his pair of pants had holes in (*its, their*) pockets.

14. Neither Sharmin nor Joy remembered to do (*their, her*) homework.

Review: Shifts in Construction

> **Underline** the incorrect pronoun and verb shifts in the following sentences. Look for shifts in person, number, voice, and tense. Correct each shift by writing the correct word or words above the underlined portion.

ride
1. Some people fly kites, while other people <u>rode</u> bicycles.

2. If you love to write, draw, paint, and act, one should probably not go into accounting.

3. Juliana hopes to go to college and planned on applying to several schools.

4. I planted zinnias and petunias in the red containers, but cosmos and sweet peas have been planted in the blue containers.

5. The students finished the essay test before he or she went to the auditorium.

6. Jack and his buddy finished his homework early and went skateboarding.

7. I walked into Grandma's kitchen and spied the dinner of your dreams.

8. There is a cricket, maybe two, who are singing in my basement.

9. The members of the class were hungry; it wanted more pizza.

10. Astronomy 406 is very difficult, and I wished I had not taken the course.

11. Does my lawn mower need a new engine, or can they be repaired?

12. When the alarm rang early on the morning of the trip, she turns it off.

13. Several of the students met to discuss his or her ACT scores.

14. Nobody really wanted to reveal how they had done on the test.

15. All Mondays are the same: fresh and challenging; most Tuesdays will be equally exciting.

16. Jan will finish her homework, and she used the rest of her time to do the laundry.

17. Neither my uncle nor his children wanted to take down his Christmas tree.

Review: Sentence Activities

Underline the simple or compound subject once and the simple or compound predicate twice in the following sentences. Then, on the line, identify the sentence as **S** for simple, **CD** for compound, **CX** for complex, or **CD-CX** for compound-complex.

_____ **1.** Although broadcasting is the most popular use of radio, it has many other uses as well.

_____ **2.** Pilots, police, and other professionals use it to communicate quickly.

_____ **3.** Scientists learn about weather by sending radio waves into the sky, and radio enthusiasts operate amateur stations all over the country.

_____ **4.** RADAR, which is a special form of radio, not only aids in the safe operation of airplanes and ships, but it also helps police departments to apprehend speeders.

Identify the underlined phrases in the following sentences as **A** for appositive, **G** for gerund, **I** for infinitive, **P** for participial, or **PREP** for prepositional.

1. Believe it or not, cooking food is something that radio waves can do well—

in a microwave oven.

2. Spies use bugs, hidden radio devices, to secretly listen to conversations.

3. Doctors can use a miniature radio transmitter enclosed in a capsule

to help them diagnose stomach ailments.

Identify the underlined clauses as adverb, adjective, or noun.

_____ **1.** Before the development of radio revolutionized communication, people had only two other means of quick, long-distance communication: the telegraph and the telephone.

_____ **2.** The drawback of both of these methods was that communication was possible only between places connected with wires, since they were required to send the signals.

_____ **3.** Radio signals, <u>which pass through the air</u>, enable people to quickly

communicate between any two points on land, sea, air—even outer

space,

_____ **4.** Radio's first practical use was for ship-to-ship and ship-to-shore

communication; operators found <u>that it aided greatly in sea rescues.</u>

Circle the correct verb in parentheses in the sentences below.

1. The cheerleading squad *(are, is)* taking the bus to the next game.

2. Either the cats or the dog *(was, were)* responsible for this mess.

3. The six o'clock news *(are, is)* coming on next.

4. Everyone in the group *(was, were)* heading for the exit at the same time.

5. There *(was, were)* an abundance of lilacs on the bushes this year.

6. Rasheed and I *(is, are)* the distance runners on our team.

7. All of the children *(are, is)* required to have their immunizations.

8. The result of the race *(are, is)* not one, but two winners.

Circle the misplaced modifier in the following sentences, and draw an arrow to the word it modifies.

1. Coffee is what most diners like with milk.

2. People need to protect their computers from viruses who use the Internet.

3. Adrian really wants a car to take to a summer concert with great speakers.

4. We tried scuba diving at a vacation resort in the lake.

5. Ricardo got a video game that enables the user to act as a pilot for his children.